Danielle reveals the power and  from the heart and through sour access the throne room of Heaven ......ure to the King of Kings. Keys are significant instruments in order to achieve access. This book will invite and give you permission to enter into the doors of your destiny.

— BECKAH SHAE, CO-FOUNDER OF SHAE SHOC RECORDS,
SINGER, SONGWRITER

Danielle Freitag, at her core, is a worshiper of Jesus. The Garden Keys leads you toward *the One* that can heal all wounds and teaches us how to seek Him even more. If you want to feel the presence of God in your reading, this book has been bathed in prayer and it seeps out through the pages.

— REBECCA BENDER, CEO & FOUNDER, RBI

There are keys of the Kingdom, keys to unlock hearts and open the floodgates of healing that wash away every chain of shame and guilt. The Father says, "Awake my Love, the nightmare is over." Read and weep, and let your tears sing the song of freedom, O Daughter of Zion.

— JAMES NESBIT, PROPHETIC ARTIST, MUSICIAN

Unlock beauty from the ashes of lies and deceit and take heart as you read about a life found in true identity and authority.

— JENNA DE JONG, CO-FOUNDER OF ACTION169 AND
WOMEN'S HEALTH ADVOCATE

In each chapter, Danielle's personal story is interlaced with words of life from the scriptures. Let yourself be intimately in touch with each key that unlocks the door as you pass through into the garden, from wounds into healing, brokenness into restoration, and from bondage into the revelation of freedom.

— Karen Krueger, Apostle, Call to The Wall,
MnAPN, HaPN

The Garden Keys is a must-read for anyone who has dealt with trauma in any form. This book will take you on a journey with King Jesus. The "keys" are imperative for the healing process. It is an encounter of the depths of Father God's love that ministers straight to the heart.

— Sarah Hacker, Hope Encounter Ministries -
Minister of Healing & Restoration

"Those who take the time to plant Danielle's words and scripture wisdom deep into their hearts will surely reap a bountiful harvest of healing and joy. So, invest the time to unearth each key she shares...because you, my friend, are worth it!"

— Keri Wilt, Author, Speaker and Co-Gardener
at FHB and Me, planting seeds of hope with her
Great-Great-Grandmother Frances Hodgson
Burnett, author of The Secret Garden

THE GARDEN KEYS

22 KEYS OF RESTORATION, VOLUME 2 -
AWAKENING DAUGHTER ZION

DANIELLE FREITAG

Cover Art & Illustrations by Anna Friendt Art and Illustration

For permission requests, quantity ordering and U.S. trade bookstores please contact the publisher at footprintpub.com or write:
Footprint Publishing, PO Box 1022, Roanoke, TX 76262

All scripture references are from the New American Standard Bible (NASB), unless otherwise noted. The New American Standard Bible (NASB) Copyright © 1960, 1962, 1963, 1968, 1971, 1972, 1973, 1975, 1977, 1995 by The Lockman Foundation.

• Scripture quotations marked (ESV) taken from The ESV® Bible (The Holy Bible, English Standard Version®). Text Edition: 2016. Copyright © 2001 by Crossway, a publishing ministry of Good News Publishers. Unauthorized reproduction of this publication is prohibited. All rights reserved.

• Scripture quotations marked (NIV) are taken from *The Holy Bible, New International Version®* NIV® Copyright © 1973, 1978, 1984, 2011 by Biblica, Inc.® Used by permission. All rights reserved worldwide.

• Scripture quotations marked (NKJV) taken from the *New King James Version®*, Copyright © 1982 by Thomas Nelson. Used by permission. All rights reserved.

• Scripture quotations marked (MSG) taken from *The Message*. Copyright© 1993, 1994, 1995, 1996, 2000, 2001, 2002. Used by permission of NavPress Publishing Group.

• Scripture quotations marked (WEB) taken from The World English Bible, which is in the Public Domain.

Adonai, from the beginning You've made a way to enter into destiny through Truth. You are my Garden.

To my dearest husband, Corey Freitag, thank you for your ongoing love and support.

To you dearest reader, to any woman who has experienced the pain of abortion, who has struggled with addiction, or who has worked in the commercial sex industry, know that you are deeply loved.

In Christ's embrace you will hear a heartbeat and find the love and freedom you long for.

Rise up Sons and Daughters
Rise up Daughter Zion

Dearest Grace,
I am beginning to hear your song.
Lightning connects us as does Trinity. This cry of longing unites Heaven and Earth. I love you and long to meet you face to face. Let's keep singing to worship King Jesus.

CONTENTS

FOREWORD

At the very moment when we each meet the Lord, we are also introduced to a secret place, a hidden sanctuary that only the two of us together know. In the Bible, that hidden, secret sanctuary is called a garden.

As we continue to grow and mature, and we come to see and hear Him better (as He also sees and hears us), we are invited to come and meet in the garden, where we can spend time together and talk face-to-face, as friends always do.

To our delight, we soon find that our garden is a carefully protected place, a peaceful refuge, complete with a private gate and our own special set of keys, where we can always go to seek a quiet place and pray.

In the Bible, those who have the keys to such a gated garden are called the Daughters of Zion. Described as special, and precious (valuable) in the sight of the Lord, these Daughters of Zion are given access to many treasures in their garden that are more valuable than diamonds and gold. These treasures are also known as wisdom, knowledge, and understanding.

For example, we learn that tears and godly sorrow may endure for the night (or even a season), but joy will surely come in the morning, and that every tear that falls during our time(s) in the barren wilderness will also bring forth new life. Nothing is wasted, all is redeemed.

We also discover that we must often wrestle (with all of our strength) for the blessings and promises of God, which are free, yet always come with a great price.

And as He gently, but oh-so-firmly, strips off the bandages and chains we were wrapped and imprisoned in, we come to discover that yes, we were also prodigals, and that we were hopelessly imprisoned, and helplessly trapped inside a great darkness.

However, during this time of intimate care and healing (therapy), we also come to recognize and trust the gentle touch of His embrace, as we find ourselves first set free, then clothed in new garments, and finally transformed into His image.

And then, as we awaken to His love, we hear Him say, "Rise up my love, my fair one, rise and shine, for your light has come!" He wants us to leave the garden, and go out into the world.

To our amazement, we also receive a new voice - to sing! - whether in times of great thanksgiving, or in times of sorrow, and especially during times of intense warfare.

In fact, we discover that we are part of a heavenly orchestra, an eternal symphony, that life itself has a sound, and that our Companion in the garden sings with us, even as He dwells in the midst of our praises.

And then, as we gain confidence and continue forward on our journey, we realize that dreams and visions often lead us and guide us toward our destiny, while His Word keeps us on the right path, as we travel through the Promised Land, which will always be a land of hills and valleys. And all the while, as the grateful Daughters of Zion, we still have the keys to the Secret Garden, which is our inheritance for all of eternity.

Amen.

Philip B. Haney
Plymouth, CA

INTRODUCTION

A Well Watered Garden

The LORD will guide you always; he will satisfy your needs in a sun-scorched land and will strengthen your frame. You will be like a well-watered garden, like a spring whose waters never fail.

Isaiah 58:11 NIV

This new season has come with a sobering reset to rise up and shake off the entanglements, whatever they may be. Priorities are being rearranged. Nothing else will suffice, but the presence of God - whatever is true, what is right, pure, and lovely. Hunger for God is a gift in this awakening that takes us deeper into the garden.

Hunger is what I've been experiencing.

As you read this second volume of *The Garden Keys - Awakening Daughter Zion*, I believe that you, too, will receive a greater hunger for God in your pursuit of Him, and through utilizing the keys from each chapter.

In the fall of 2018, also the start of the Hebrew year 5779, I spent much needed time alone with the Lord. This meant shutting out distractions. Making a way into the garden, the secret place, has meant intentional time in the living Word of God. I became painfully aware that anything superficial, or false, was being stripped away. The motivation for choices was exposed. Anything I was doing that wasn't honoring to my own body, spirit, or soul, or honoring to God, would no longer be something I was able to take part in. What seemed like such a small thing became a recognized thistle that would not be allowed to grow.

Without asking Him for a word as I typically do in the new year, I was led to pursue Him - the man, the divine, Jesus Christ the Messiah. I didn't want a word, I wanted Him. In pursuit of Him, I felt His embrace.

The word *embrace*, chabaq in Hebrew, is mentioned 13 times in scripture and is related to embracing a loved one, a season, or wisdom.

To embrace Jesus, and to allow His embrace, I've had to learn to follow His leading. Turning away from opportunities that initially appear as good has come with an abundance of blessing. When we learn to say no based on His leading, wisdom is embraced.

In the restoration process of sober living, learning to follow His leading has brought joy, but the journey has also come with pain. Most often, however, I am greeted with deeper encounters with God and greater rivers of peace, no matter the circumstances. For each one of us who is on a journey of restoration, we must protect our time, the mind, and priorities. In the process, like the Samaritan woman spoken of in John 4, we learn what it means to wait, to thirst, and to be presented with a choice. We can encounter a *real love that quenches thirst*. In essence, our desert places can be met with life.

For fear of their spiteful judgement, the Samaritan woman waited to draw water from the well until the other women had left. Instead of going in the morning, she went to draw water in the middle of the day. In the desert, in the place of her shame, she encountered the Messiah.

In the story, Jesus rests at Jacob's well, weary from His own journey. Jacob's well at Shechem was situated between two mountains - Mt. Gerizim (Blessing), and Mt. Ebal (Curses). This was the place where the Samaritan woman met the Messiah and was embraced by real love. Nothing was hidden. Jesus embraced the Samaritan woman and told her about a living water that would give her freedom from having to search, to seek, or to be seduced by the ways of the world. She stood in a place between the old way of life and the new, and was given a choice and a chance to drink from the living water, not the dead.

Far too often, we also find ourselves between the two, and yet, there is only one source of life to draw from, one mountain to run to, and One to embrace who embraces us back. He leads us into the garden of blessings where we drink from the fountain of living water.

I've been embracing what is blossoming for me in this season, and I encourage you to do the same. Be vulnerable enough to allow His leading, which chips away at any false identity and pulls up the weeds that come with affirmation of self through superficial pursuits. On the straight road into the garden, each one of us is brought to the place where nothing is hidden, and where we can, in fact, encounter *real love*.

Give yourself permission to embrace what He is doing within you, a new thing that is beautiful, like a seed planted in good soil turning into cascading roses that reach for the light.

You don't have to do what others are doing. You don't have to do the thing that seems like it's all the hype. Freedom is experienced when you're in His embrace and He gives you direction and refreshment. Embrace the process. Embrace this season. Embrace wisdom.

Most of all, embrace Jesus, and let Him embrace you. For those of you who pursue Him and turn away from what is vile, the wells of abundance are open.

A dangerous prayer to pray is, "Lord, refine me, define me as

Yours. Whatever it takes, remove the idols and the false ideas of self. Keep me away from placing my value upon what is superficial and from comparison that distracts. You are the only One who affirms me. I find my purpose in You. Cause a hunger within me for You, the Living Water, which is Your Word."

Invite Holy Spirit into your time of reading *The Garden Keys*. In doing so, you will be taken deeper into the garden. Each key is biblical, and when utilized, can cause awakening that ignites hunger for God. Learn more about yourself, and how you were wonderfully made in the image of God, for God, with a purpose and unique destiny by His good design.

In Volume 1 of *The Garden Keys, The Beginning to Israel*, you were brought through the realities of the modern-day entanglements and given thirteen keys for restoration to move into the garden of your life.

In Volume 2 of *The Garden Keys, Awakening Daughter Zion*, continue to take an in-depth look into the commercial sex industry and what fuels the industry, in an authentic, real-life journey out of the depths of grief from abortion, addiction and the business of exploitation.

Come out of the thorns and thistles of entanglement, and move into the garden of your life as you apply biblical keys for restoration in a journey that comes around full circle, back to the garden. The secret is no longer a secret anymore.

There is One who leads you into the garden with loving chords of kindness, that place of meeting face-to-face where you become a well-watered garden. All of creation waits eagerly for the glory of the children of God – you.

This is the awakening.

Dear Reader, this is the second of two volumes of *The Garden Keys, 22 Keys of Restoration*. The two volumes are a set that will lead you from The Beginning to Israel, then on to Awakening Daughter Zion.

PROLOGUE

You were in a field wearing this gorgeous white dress, almost like a wedding dress. And you were twirling with such freedom.
All of a sudden, the picture faded.
When it became clear again you were dancing, but this time not as free and the dress was a little frayed and torn.
All of a sudden, Jesus came towards you.

When He embraced you, and you allowed the embrace, everything else faded. When you looked into His eyes, your dress became white. Suddenly, you realized He'd created you clean, holy, and pure. Like in the beginning, before the violations, the addictions, or the greatest heartache, in His embrace you became childlike with freedom.

In the waiting of refinement and fulfillment of promise, God cleaned you up. He is removing the names of the false idols from your mouth and out of your life. Not only are you beginning to recognize what these false idols are, but you are also being awakened to tune in to God's strategic sound that orchestrates an army to move in unity.

Moving forward in this awakening, we are each being tuned to God's strategic sound, a sound that causes unity and brings healing. This sound unites Heaven and Earth as many unite their song to the cry of the eternals.

Women and mothers alike arise to sing the song that unites them with the eternals. Sons and daughters tune in to a sound that shakes Heaven and all of earth into the full realization that we've been brought into the garden, just like in the beginning.

We come full circle back to the garden in covenant - back to the beginning, in the greatest love story ever told.

The garden is a secret and safe place where life blossoms. Judgements of self fade away. Insecurities fed by superficial pursuits do not exist. We soon come to realize that in the garden our waste places are comforted, our wilderness is like Eden, and the desert is like the garden of the Lord. Joy and gladness are found in us, thanksgiving and songs of melody unite Heaven and Earth in a convergence point that thunders like the heartbeat of God.

In time, destiny unfolds to bring the bride and the Bridegroom together. The song and dance of awakening has begun. There is One who leads, and one who follows, until the two are like one.

He began to dance with you. At first you wouldn't look at Him
but then He took your face in His hands and gazed into your eyes.
When He did, your dress became white again and it was new.

THE GARDEN
עֵדֶן

1

DECLARE FREEDOM DAUGHTER ZION

DECLARATION KEY

Shake yourself from the dust, rise up, O captive Jerusalem; Loose yourself from the chains around your neck, O captive daughter of Zion.

Isaiah 52:2

Years after getting out of the Iron Furnace, I had extremely vivid dreams about being back in the strip club. Because I was living a new life painted in color, I hated having those black dreams of seduction.

In the dreams, I played the part of seductive Shannon, just as I was taught.

After waking up, I would try to go back to sleep. Once asleep, the dream would continue true to where it had left off. As the dream played out in story form, waking up and falling asleep would happen several times.

With a black, skin-tight outfit, little was left to the imagination, but this is how we all dressed in the club. My face covered in heavy makeup, feet fitted with crystal clear heals for sex appeal, I carried a stack of cash with the hundreds on the outside to show my worth. Not having money in my hands meant the embarrassment of rejection.

The club in the dream was all too familiar.

This was the place I knew by heart, every space from top to bottom, including the two stages, beds, and couch dance rooms. Recognizable sounds carried throughout the club, and the same exact lights shone bright in that night life.

The only thing different was the dressing room.

Instead of what I remembered, what I saw in the dream was a type of cattle barn without the dirt or animals enclosed. Each girl had her place to get ready. Each *stall* contained a mirror and vanity counter top where she would keep her makeup, hairspray, body mist, and curling iron. Girls were dashing in and out of the locker area, changing outfits and preparing themselves for their next customer or stage set.

In the dream, it was significant to let the DJ know what songs to play. The sound made all the difference for the dance. It always does. The song, as usual, was *Orestes or Judith* by A Perfect Circle. The dream displayed scenes of being back in the dressing room to prepare for a seductive performance on stage. Suddenly, one of the tall managers who carried extra pounds of weight began speaking out harsh commands in the direction of one of the girls. With his arm raised high, about to impact a hard blow, his voice caused fear that demanded attention.

While seeing this vulgar display of power, I stormed towards him on a mission of righteous anger, stilettos and all. Instead of pushing him as intended, I gravitated towards one of the girls to bring protection.

In that moment, a cell phone appeared in my hands.

Frantic to call for help, I dialed the numbers: 911...911...911. I was trying to call my dad, which represented calling God, the Father. I had no voice and could not speak.

While dialing 911 in the dream, I heard the words "Declare Freedom." In reality, as I was dreaming, again I heard an audible voice, "Declare Freedom."

Startled in the depths of my spirit, in a good way, I woke up and spoke out the words as a declaration. With a loud voice, in the dark of my bedroom, I *declared freedom*. Because of what I had been learning in my Bible, and because of what Holy Spirit was leading me to do, I also said the name of Jesus several times.

The dream came months after my South Africa restoration, written about in Volume 1 of *The Garden Keys, The Beginning to Israel*. That dream was one of many in the midst of getting sober and going back to college to pursue what had been planted in the good soil of my heart.

Feeling as though there was an electric current moving through my body, I shouted loudly to declare freedom for the girl in the dream. She was so entangled in the web of the industry that she couldn't find her way out. That feeling of being trapped was once familiar to me. The 911 dream awakened me to the power of speaking in agreement with God's Word, not only for myself, but also in intercession for others. This was an awakening dream to speak up in sound, and eventually in song.

Once trapped in a corrupt system that altered my thinking, it took belief, action and vocal agreement with truth to separate from captivity, referenced to as Egypt - The Iron Furnace. It took understanding God-given dreams and visions, vocalizing an out loud agreement with the Word of God, and recognizing entanglements that would keep me from the straight road that would otherwise bring entrance into the garden.

Finding and utilizing the keys to flourish in the garden of each of our lives also means recognizing what will keep us from the Promised Land. The opposite of the Promised Land is Babylon, which reflects a corrupt world system that is roaring and raging in lust and drunkenness. Egypt can be likened to Babylon and the involvement of compromise.

Loosing myself from the captivity that haunted me in the night meant tuning my ears to a different sound and dancing to a different dance. No one else was going to do it for me. And yet, led by the Holy Spirit, I would speak up and declare the living Word out loud. The living Word of God brings change, "For the word of God is living and active and sharper than any two-edged sword, and piercing as far as the division of soul and spirit, of both joints and marrow, and able to judge the thoughts and intentions of the heart" (Hebrews 4:12).

Jesus Himself is the Living Word, and the One who is drawing each one of us into the Promised Land - the garden.

Understanding a Babylon System

As Shannon, I painted on the face, strapped on the heels, and shut down my heart. I was dead inside. Falling deeper into the grips of a progressive and fatal addiction, I looked forward to the next high and dreaded the next low. I had been seduced into the Iron Furnace that served a different god than the God of Abraham, Isaac and Jacob who I had learned about as a little girl.

Slavery works by subtle deception that progresses to cross the boundary lines. Slavery to the wrong master can cause entanglements in thistles and thorns. There are places that perpetuate deceit, and I had been in one of them - The Iron Furnace of the strip club industry, which is a part of the web of the commercial sex industry that profits from the sale of souls.

A loving forewarning to any woman reading this chapter who has worked in the commercial sex industry, or who may be working in the strip club industry now: Know that you are deeply loved, treasured and honored in my sight, and in God's. The truth is, we can become "destroyed for lack of knowledge" (see Hosea 4:6) and so, I write the following from my own experience, time out of the industry in sobriety, and study of the scriptures. It is my deepest hope and prayer that each one of us better understands the difference between the Kingdom of God, the Garden, and the Promised Land, and that of Babylon that manifests as a corrupt and immoral world system that seeks to enslave us.

In Bible history, Babylon is tied to ancient Babel, which is mentioned in Genesis 11. In Babel, people built a tower to declare themselves godlike, which resulted in their scattering and the different languages found throughout the world today.

When the Bible tells of Satan's attempt to establish his visible kingdom on earth we are given a picture of a woman as Babylon, like a city that sits on seven mountains (see Revelation 17:9). The figurative Babylon that is written about is not only a city, but a one-world system that opposes God and His remnant people. This system, a machine that has working parts, exerts mind control to manifest every kind of lust, greed and deception within those who are influenced.

From reading Revelation 17, we see that before the fall of Babylon, called "the great mother of prostitutes and of earth's abominations," we are given a picture and description of Babylon that describes, "the judgment of the great harlot who sits on many waters, with whom the kings of the earth committed acts of immorality, and those who dwell on the earth were made drunk with the wine of her immorality." The scriptures tell us that those who are drunk in sexual lust are literally drinking from a cup that is intoxicating, because it is Babylon's cup. This is not a good intoxication, but a diluting, toxic, and dangerous one.

The book of Judges opens with the Israelites in the land which God promised to them. In that time, however, they worshiped "foreign gods" instead of God:

> Then the sons of Israel again did evil in the sight of the Lord, served the Baals and the Ashtaroth, the gods of Aram, the gods of Sidon, the gods of Moab, the gods of the sons of Ammon, and the gods of the Philistines; *thus they forsook the Lord and did not serve Him.* (Judges 10:6, *emphasis mine*)

In the club, the Iron Furnace, unknown to me at that time, I had been groomed into serving the same idols that the Israelites once served when they went astray. Look at the connection between the vast commercial sex industry and what the prophet Samuel wrote in the book of Judges.

First of all, God, whose name is Yahweh (YHVH), cherishes us as His bride. He has the best plan for our lives in the greatest love story. We are His beloved bride who He has created for communion and to have dominion over the earth. He is the faithful Husband who leads us in a good way: "For your husband is your Maker, whose name is the LORD of hosts; and your Redeemer is the Holy One of Israel, Who is called the God of all the earth" (Isaiah 54:5).

The name "Baal" means *husband*. God references the name Baal when the Israelites, His chosen people, were bowing to and worshiping these false idols. He knew it would be dangerous and devastating to the ones He loved when they served other gods, so He brought a wake up call. The word "Baal" also means *owner* or *task master*, which refers to being controlled by, or being in bondage (slavery).

One of the most prominent idols that Israel worshipped was Asherah. The first mention of the Asherah pole is in Exodus 34:13 (NIV): "Break down their altars, smash their sacred stones and cut down their Asherah poles." Asherah was one of the goddesses of fertility who was popular throughout the ancient near east. The term Asherah can refer to either the deity or the objects that represent her worship, which were wooden poles or cut pillars that stood at places of worship to bring honor.

The names for Asherah have varied through different groups. The Canaanites called her Asherah. In Ugaritic literature she is referred to as "The Lady Asherah of the Sea." The Babylonians called her Astarte, a Greek name. Astarte embodies both sexual and war-like attributes. She is arguably the merging of Canaanite idols with the Babylonian/Assyrian goddess Ishtar. Astarte and Asherah carry the name "Queen of Heaven" (see Exodus 20:4; Jeremiah 7:18, 44:17-19).

When I came out of the sex industry and the grips of addiction, I began creating vision boards to set goals and get a word from the Lord to catch His vision. I'll never forget cutting out the word "goddess" and placing it on my vision board. After reading the scriptures and encountering Holy Spirit's leading, I was led to take that word off my vision board when I learned about the "Queen of Heaven." With good biblical knowledge, we are less likely to be seduced by the enemy's tactics for attention to self.

Asherahs were common in the land of Israel when worship of this goddess was popular. Both Ahab and Jezebel worshipped Asherah along with their worship of Baal (see 1 Kings 16:33; 1 Kings 18:19). At least four hundred prophets of Asherah were part of Jezebel's home.

If you look up pictures of Asherah, you'll likely see a woman statue depicted with her shirt off. In both aspects of Baal and Asherah worship there was a quest for fame, power, and beauty, and a display of perverse sex. Both idols were fertility gods and the people who would offer worship towards them produced children, who they actually sacrificed for power. Keep in mind, these are false gods, otherwise known as demons or principalities connected to Babylon (Satan) who seeks to win the allegiance of people through deception and compromise.

Consider what was done for demonic idols: Immoral and perverted sex was the main focus of the false gods, and the act of prostitution was their worship. Sex with temple prostitutes or orgies was an act of inspiring the gods. Asherah groves are mentioned over forty times in scripture and some scholars believe that certain types of trees, like poles, were set up as altars. These trees were carved into forms of the female body and were a gathering place for orgies and dancing.

Are there any alarms going off in your spirit yet?

Does this remind you of anything?

In Deuteronomy 16:21 the Lord says, "You shall not plant for yourself an Asherah of any kind of tree beside the altar of the Lord your God, which you shall make for yourself." God said this because the ancient tree poles were used to dance around and entice men into sexual worship to Baal as they were placed next to the altar of Baal. God didn't want His people to perish for lack of knowledge by offering worship to demonic principalities.

It is important to note that sex was created by God. Sex is to be experienced within the perfect boundary lines of marriage as a means of covenant, reproduction, and enjoyment, between a man and a woman. He is jealous in love for His bride and desires her safety and well-being, and so, He will cause a wake up call if needed.

When a new altar of worship (*bowing down, submitting to*) is built to offer praise to the God of Israel, other altars of worship to false idols will perish, or burn.

"For I am confident of this very thing, that He who began a good work in you will perfect it until the day of Christ Jesus." (Philippians 1:6)

Seduction as a Deceiving Tactic

Smooth talk, pupils dilated from the pills, long dark hair and a curvy body were my selling points. I was taught by the invisible, but very real demonic Asherahs that came in the form of what the sex industry instructed. The teachings came by various forms of influences, including by the man and the substances that groomed me into the industry. Exposure to those influences was just one of the entanglements that gripped me tightly. Grief in the darkest form, a secret to be kept, had blackened my soul.

There is a Babylon culture that is teaching generations of young women to be glamorous and seductive as taught by pictures in magazines and movies, including pornography. Sadly, the glorification of hyper-sexuality has been brought to us by superstars like Madonna and Beyonce, who are both highly influenced by the above mentioned principalities.

Authors and revolutionary leaders Jon and Jolene Hamill capture some of the current trends in our hyper-sexualized culture in their book *Crown and Throne*. Hamill writes, "Both Madonna and Beyonce performed sexually explicit acts featuring Masonic and Illuminati symbolism, with direct expressions of worship to Baal and the gods of Egypt."[1] In his accurate description, Hamill was referring to the halftime shows that so many watched during the annual Super Bowls.

If you're awake, it doesn't take much to see the blatant and direct worship of these idols in our culture. A strip club, and all that goes on within its web, is part of the Babylonian system that gives worship to Baal and Asherah - demonic principalities that seduce people into lust, greed, and false fame.

Clearly, Babylon and the Promised Land are two totally different places that come with different lifestyles. One exploits and the other shows honor. One is not safe, but the other protects. One gives worship to demons while the other gives worship to the one true God, Yahweh, the God of Israel. It is that black and white, and grace meets us in between as we seek the One worthy of praise.

The alarms of awakening are going off now before too many become so drunk on lust they can't hear the voice of the One who created them, and who desires to lead them in a better way.

The reality is those who exchange money for a moment of sexual pleasure are taking part in drinking from the cup of Babylon.

A few more facts about Babylon:

Babylon exposes for profit (Revelation 18:9)
Babylon grows rich from the power of her luxurious living (Revelation 18:3)
Babylon seduces people into sexual immorality (Revelation 18:3)
Babylon is drunk on porn

Babylon sells souls - people (Revelation 18:13)

Babylon is drunk with the blood of the saints (Revelation 17:6)

Babylon dishonors and seeks to exploit the sons and daughters of God

Babylon is a dwelling place for demons (Revelation 18:2)

Not all in Israel gave in to the worship of Asherah. In fact, there were those who stood against these idols. These people were reformers and pioneers who demonstrated they were only going to worship the one true God, the God of Israel. Elijah challenged both the prophets of Baal and Asherah in 1 Kings 18. Josiah destroyed the items that were set apart for the worship of Asherah and Baal (see 2 Chronicles 34:3-4). Gideon became the first to fight against the infestation of Asherah poles (see Judges 6:25-27).

In this time of awakening, there are many rising up like Elijah and Josiah who are radical enough to worship the one true, living God, Yahweh, the God of Israel. It's likely that you are one of those radical reformers called to the frontlines, even if you've been caught up in the grips of addiction or the sex industry in the past as I once was.

Justice Awakening

Chapter 52 of Isaiah has come alive for me in the years of my restoration journey. The opening verses startle me to attention:

Awake, awake, Clothe yourself in your strength, O Zion; Clothe yourself in your beautiful garments, O Jerusalem, the holy city; For the uncircumcised and the unclean will no longer come into you. Shake yourself from the dust, rise up, O captive Jerusalem; Loose yourself from the chains around your neck, O captive daughter of Zion. (Isaiah 52:1-2)

In other words, wake yourself up with the Word of God and

know who you are as royalty. Declare the living Word out loud. You are not meant to be a slave to the entanglements of Babylon that come to seduce and tempt. Rise up, embrace Jesus, and allow Him to embrace you. Shake yourself from the dust. Come out of the things that keep you captive. Be free to take the yoke of the Lord God of Israel, for He says to you: "My yoke is easy and My burden is light" (Matthew 11:30). His way is so much better than being yoked with Baal.

A yoke is a wooden beam that can be used between a pair of oxen to enable them to work together to pull a plow or cart. Animals that are yoked together are closely joined and must move together. A yoke is used as a symbol for alliance or union.

Daughter Zion follows the way of the Lord God, knowing that He leads to life and not death. Further instruction in the book of Isaiah is to, "Depart, depart, go out from there, touch nothing unclean; Go out of the midst of her, purify yourselves, you who carry the vessels of the Lord" (Isaiah 52:11). Coming out of "there" means coming out of Babylon.

These commands in Isaiah are sobering reminders of the need to be awake and to know that in Christ, God has "raised us up with Him, and seated us with Him in the heavenly places in Christ Jesus" (Ephesians 2:6).

Awake! Awake! Rouse yourself awake to "Loose the chains of injustice and untie the cords of the yoke to set the oppressed free" (see Isaiah 58:6).

Declare Freedom Daughter Zion

According to Romans 10:9, one enters into covenant with Jesus Christ through belief and verbalization: "...if you confess with your mouth Jesus as Lord, and believe in your heart that God raised Him from the dead, you will be saved." It was God who woke me up in the middle of the night telling me to *declare freedom*. This is the season of awakening in the midnight hour for many of us.

He has extended His hand to bring each one of us out of the

Iron Furnace, but there is always a choice whether or not to follow His lead. One thing is for sure, I had to be the one to decide to leave, but it was by His doing. It is "by His doing you are in Christ Jesus, who became to us wisdom from God, and righteousness and sanctification, and redemption" (1 Corinthians 1:30).

He begins to bring transformation and change that reflects His character. His leading ignites passion within us to honor and worship the only One deserving of worship. His presence empowers us to protect the gates of our lives.

Protecting the Gates of Body, Spirit and Soul

It is necessary to protect the gates of our own garden if we desire a life of spiritual and physical wellness - body, spirit and soul. Gates to the body include the eyes, ears, nose, mouth, and skin. The soul, which is your mind, will, and emotions, can be influenced by what enters through the gates of your body.

Several years ago, I discovered a social media post that went something like this: "If you are religious or sensitive, do not look at this post." The picture resembled a man and woman posing as though they were having sex. What that person shared on social media was toxic. I blocked her posts, but kept the communication lines open. In the midst of her battle, she reached out to talk with me about her struggles with viewing pornography. Interestingly, God had been leading me to pray for her. For the first time, she was able to tell someone what was going on. Silence would no longer be betrayal.

In Matthew we are told, "The eye is the lamp of the body; so then if your eye is clear, your whole body will be full of light. But if your eye is bad, your whole body will be full of darkness. If then the light that is in you is darkness, how great is the darkness!" (Matthew 6:22-23)

It's not about being "too religious" if we choose not to look at something, especially if it's pornographic. Protecting ourselves produces honor for self, others and God. We are better able to commune with God through prayer when our minds are not bogged down with images that distract. Greater intimacy with God the Father results in perfect peace.

In scripture, King David says, "I will not look with approval on anything that is vile. I hate what faithless people do; I will have no part in it" (Psalm 101:3 NIV). David wanted to live a blameless life, although he fell short, as we all do, David knew to look at God, to seek Him, and God honored him. The Messiah came through David's lineage.

In today's culture, we are literally surrounded by vile things, which is why we must protect our eyes. Visions of vile things enter in the gates of the eyes through movies, television shows, and the internet. As followers of Christ, it is important that we protect our eyes so that we do not come into agreement with the very same spirit that is fueling the sex industry, which is all connected to Babylon. When pornography is viewed, there is a partnership formed with the same spirits that are fueling sex trafficking.

As those who say we are in the fight against exploitation and trafficking, we must be the ones who are protecting our eye gates from what is perverse.

What is allowed through the eye gates enters into the mind. What enters into the mind affects the words we declare, which ultimately, effects behavior.

May there be a fight for the eyes!

Make war on the tactics of culture that seek to annihilate. Be aware of the amount of television that is consumed, the types of shows that are being watched and the false or fake news being downloaded.

Being "desensitized" is dangerous, a sure tactic of Babylon.

In my dream, as I stood in that dressing room dialing 911, it was not only for the precious daughters of the living God. That 911 call was also for the men and women who enter into the strip clubs to drink from the cup of Babylon. That 911 call was also for the club managers who are themselves like puppets being controlled by an evil puppet master. The key was to declare truth, to speak up and speak out.

911! 911!

Emergency! Emergency!

There is a culture that is drinking from the wrong cup. The world's strip club industry is drunk in seduction and alluring millions to drink from Babylon's cup. And yet, there is also a remnant of people who are waking up. As we return to the Lord, we become free from any kind of bondage or slavery. We begin to declare truth and receive a new name, Daughter Zion. As we learn who we really are, and Whose we are, we are being delivered from that which rages against us.

> Then Samuel spoke to all the house of Israel, saying, "If you return to the Lord with all your heart, remove the foreign gods and the Ashtaroth from among you and direct your hearts to the Lord and serve Him alone; and He will deliver you from the hand of the Philistines." (1 Samuel 7:3)

DECLARATION KEY

1. What does the 911 call refer to in this chapter?

2. What did you learn about Babylon, Asherah and Baal? After learning this, where in our culture can you see the worship of these idols taking place?

3. Is there anything that you want to change after reading this chapter?

4. Spend some time meditating on Isaiah 52. Write out all of Isaiah 52 in a journal.

5. What Scriptures as declarations from this chapter can you speak out loud now?

Father God,

Thank You for awakening me to better understand the significance of my actions. Cause in me a desire to honor You in all that I do. Thank You for the greatest Counselor of all, who leads me and guides me into all truth, the Holy Spirit. Lord, would You cause an increase in discernment within so that I am awake and aware. Thank You for Your Word, a lamp and light for me.

In the name of Jesus, Amen.

2

A NEW NAME

IDENTITY KEY

*Whoever has ears, let them hear what the Spirit says to the
churches. To the one who is victorious, I will give some of the
hidden manna. I will also give that person a white stone with a
new name written on it, known only to the one who receives it.*

Revelation 2:17 NIV

The evening sunset was one of the most unique I had ever seen. It
was late February and the week prior the weather patterns
permitted running outside without a jacket, gloves or even a
stocking cap. Snowfall brought us a fresh 12 inches of white that
covered the surface of everything in sight.

That was the day I saw the fingerprint.

As we drove north to catch our flight, I caught a glimpse of the
clouds that resembled fingerprints. Although my husband was
obsessing about the fish he was planning to catch on our

Caribbean vacation, I eagerly alerted him to the miracle. I wanted him to experience the uniqueness that God had painted for us. Corey had been reading up on various kinds of fish, but was willing to pause for just a moment to look towards the sky.

Tiny, perfect little groves were painted by white clouds in front of a blue sky. The clouds were telling of things to come. As I marveled at the cloud fingerprints, I was reminded of the little girl Corey had a vision of while we were in Israel.

Becoming lost in the sunset's beauty, I couldn't help but thank God for His exceptional designs, perfectly woven together and complete. White clouds touched with pink and red tones filled the sky and thoughts of a baby's fingerprint formed in my thoughts. The words of Malachi pierced my mind.

Was this the fingerprint of our someday Hannah, or perhaps Malachi? Suddenly, I proclaimed with full confidence, "We're going to have a baby."

Smiling from ear to ear, Corey again looked up from his fishing lesson. Our eyes locked with one another, creating a space for hope and expectation. Nothing more needed to be said. As our drive continued north there was a confirming peace about the identities of our children. There was something prophetic about the fingerprints that would forever be embedded on my heart.

When something is *prophetic,* it is a type of foretelling of events. To be prophetic is to be God's mouthpiece - to speak from God's perspective. The most obvious definition of prophecy is to speak the words of God, which happens in relationship, because He gives us His Holy Spirit. Most current understanding of the prophetic is that it is foretelling of what is to come. In other words, to prophesy is to say what will happen in the future as inspired by Holy Spirit knowledge.

Personal prophecies may relate to the future of our lives and our spheres of influence, including our family, our city, and may even extend to the nations. For Corey and I, we know we are called to pray for Israel, but we've also been given a heart for China through a series of divine confirmations, prophecies given by trusted prophets, personal visions, and words from the Lord.

More important than prophecy, is understanding identity.

Name Significance

My husband's name "Corey" means *God's peace* and *prosperous*. Psalm 1:3 is a related scripture to his name, which has to do with being prosperous. My prayer momma's name "Ruth" means *friend*, which is very fitting. Our good friends, also ministry co-founders along with us, named their baby Leo. Leo was the name given to them when they prayed about a name and it is a significant name for this season for many reasons.

"Leo" means *lion*.

A name is that by which a person, place or thing is marked and known. In scripture, names were generally descriptive of the person, their position, a circumstance, or a hope entertained concerning them.

A dear friend named Annie recently sent information about my name, which led to my excitement in learning what my own name means. Before learning more about my name, God had been revealing the letters of the "aleph-bet," the Hebrew alphabet, to me during my times of study and prayer. The scripture related to my name is Psalm 119:112: "I have inclined my heart to perform Your statutes forever, even to the end."

This Psalm is arranged in a pattern. There are 22 letters in the Hebrew alphabet, and Psalm 119 contains 22 units of eight verses each. Each of the 22 sections is given to a letter of the Hebrew alphabet and each line in that section begins with that letter. Psalm 119 tells us that to know the creator God we must know His law, ordinances, word, commandments, statutes, precepts, decrees, testimonies, ways, and faithfulness.

Read that last sentence again.

My name, Danielle, means *God is my judge*, which is comforting. It used to be alarming until I better understood who God is through reading the scriptures and spending time with Him. His leading and judgements as the one true and just Judge tell me that He is not only fighting for me, but that He is the only one whose judgement matters.

Daniel gives account of a vision of God as a judge: "I kept looking until thrones were set up, and the Ancient of Days took His seat; His vesture was like white snow and the hair of His head like pure wool. His throne was ablaze with flames, its wheels were a burning fire. A river of fire was flowing and coming out from before Him; Thousands upon thousands were attending Him, and myriads upon myriads were standing before Him; The court sat, and the books were opened" (Daniel 7:9-10).

The book of Daniel is more exciting, and more worth praying and pressing into, than any TV show or distraction that seeks our attention to desensitize us. God's throne has wheels - and not just wheels, but fire! His vesture is like white snow!

He is my judge, just as He is your only judge, and He sees life through Jesus Christ, whose life I am hidden within as told in Colossians: "For you have died and your life is hidden with Christ in God" (Colossians 3:3). To be hidden is to be in the secret place, concealed, or even undercover. Your life in Christ is hidden, safe, and concealed.

There is mention of a book of life in the scriptures in which names are recorded (see Daniel 12:1; Revelation 3:5). There is also a book of remembrance being written when God's people come together and talk:

> Then those who feared the Lord spoke to one another, and the Lord gave attention and heard it, and a book of remembrance was written before Him for those who fear the Lord and who esteem His name. "They will be Mine," says the Lord of hosts, "on the day that I prepare My own possession, and I will spare them as a man spares his own son who serves him." So you will again distinguish between the righteous and the wicked, between

one who serves God and one who does not serve Him. (Malachi 3:16-18)

Clearly there are records in Heaven, including books and scrolls that are still to be written. I'll never forget the dream I had in which I saw open books with blank pages. The dream ended with a large noise like the sound of a judge's gavel coming down in finality.

The psalmist even tells of a book in which all of our days are written about:

> My frame was not hidden from You, when I was made in secret, and skillfully wrought in the depths of the earth; Your eyes have seen my unformed substance; And in Your book were all written the days that were ordained for me, when as yet there was not one of them. (Psalm 139:15-16)

Your life, your name, and your very frame is known by God. Knowing your identity in Christ is a key towards restoration. You were woven together in the secret and hidden place with a purpose ordained especially for you.

Do you know what your name means?

In biblical times, a name reflected character and the person's anticipated mission, which may have turned out for either good or ill. A name may embody the spiritual vision of parents for their child's future or may be prophetic of future outcomes. Some parents seek God for a name while their baby is hidden in the womb, but known by God. Perhaps there is a name that is passed on through the family lineage, or it could simply be that a name is liked and agreed upon by the parents.

When Jacob, son of Isaac, was in his nineties, God changed his name to Israel as a token of blessing. In fact, twice God assured Jacob of his new name. Jacob wrestled in such a way that showed perseverance, so God blessed him with a new name.

God responded to Jacob by saying, "Your name shall no longer be called Jacob, but Israel, for you have striven with God and with men, and have prevailed" (Genesis 32:28). After this divine wrestling match in which Jacob wrestled for a blessing face-to-face with God, he was in fact blessed. It is likely Jacob did not have a full understanding of the significance of the new name, but he knew what happened was sacred. He called the name of the place where he was blessed "Peniel," which means *the face of God.*

When was the last time you wrestled for a blessing, or to know your identity?

This story of Jacob receiving a new name speaks volumes about not only persistence over a matter, but that God's response was to give Jacob a new name as a blessing. In the face of God, we learn who we really are.

Later in scripture, Jacob responds to challenging situations with just actions, leading the people away from what could eventually harm them - false idol worship. "So Jacob said to his household and to all who were with him, 'Put away the foreign gods which are among you, and purify yourselves and change your garments'" (Genesis 35:2). He further responded to God's leading after the defilement of his daughter and response of his sons towards their sister's humiliation of being taken to bed without being wed. Simeon and Levi, Dinah's brothers, killed the one who defiled their sister, as well his father and all of the males in the city. Taking a woman to bed was to consummate a marriage. If there was sex before marriage, it was a significant humiliation.

Jacob's response to difficult times was to arise, worship and remember all the times that God had been faithful. Not only did he remember God, but he also remembered his identity, *Israel.* Even though he would wrestle, he would prevail, face-to-face with God.

A new identity in Christ will take wrestling, reading the scriptures and taking time in prayer to hear from God. When we learn who we really are and Whose we are, we will not desire the things of Babylon that remind us of the old self who was once in bondage.

Shortly after I came out of the industry and drug addiction, there was a time when I burned items that represented the past. As I learned about being a new creation in Christ, clothes from the strip club along with other items were burned. When I refused to let go of the new joy I had found in Christ and in reading His Word, there came blessing. When I was empowered to make a better choice, there came health.

A cleansing of the past comes with a fire that purifies.

You will be Given a New Name

There are predestined sons and daughters who God knows are His special possession, His chosen inheritance. You, dear one, are His chosen one who will receive a new name. You will overcome, because He first overcame death and deceit.

Jesus creates within you a new identity that is righteous, holy, and clean. Any name you've ever been called that is negative is a lie. Begin to replace the lies with truth. Ask God for an understanding of *who you are*. In correspondence to asking, meditate on these scriptures about a new name:

> He who has an ear, let him hear what the Spirit says to the churches. To him who overcomes, to him I will give some of the hidden manna, and I will give him a white stone, and a new name written on the stone which no one knows but he who receives it. (Revelation 2:17)

> The nations will see your righteousness, and all kings your glory; And you will be called by a new name which the mouth of the Lord will designate. (Isaiah 62:2)

> But you are a chosen race, a royal priesthood, a holy nation, a people for God's own possession, so that you may proclaim the excellencies of Him who has called you out of darkness into His marvelous light. (1 Peter 2:9)

> He who overcomes, I will make him a pillar in the temple of My God, and he will not go out from it anymore; and I will write on

him the name of My God, and the name of the city of My God, the new Jerusalem, which comes down out of heaven from My God, and My new name. (Revelation 3:12)

Jesus bestows on you:

1. A new name known only to you
2. The name of God
3. The New Jerusalem, which comes down from Heaven
4. Jesus' new name

Scripture makes it very clear that those of us who believe in Jesus Christ are given a new name by God Himself. No matter what anyone has called you or what your name is now, whether you like its meaning or not, you're going to receive a new name known only to you.

Your Life is Hidden in Truth

In the book of John we learn, "In the beginning was the Word, and the Word was with God, and the Word was God. He was in the beginning with God" (John 1:1-2). Jesus was with God in the beginning and He is complete, the perfect expression of the truth.

And you will know the truth, and the truth will make you free. (John 8:32)

The Greek word for *truth* is "alethia," which means *in truth, according to truth* and *in fact.* Truth also refers to reality. In reality, Jesus was with God in the beginning. There was a plan in place long before Satan brought deceit to Adam and Eve. We know this by studying the scriptures and especially by digging into the Hebrew meaning of words.

Throughout Jewish history, the Israelites have held onto the truth that their deepest selves never entered exile. Inner self, or *inner being*, never entered captivity (drug addiction, exploitation), which is why there was struggle. Inner self would never authorize slavery or death.

Keep in mind, we are made of body, spirit and soul, created in His image.

Think about it this way: there was already an overcoming of deceit through the life and blood of Jesus Christ. In John we learn about Jesus that He was with God in the beginning and that, "All things came into being through Him, and apart from Him nothing came into being that has come into being" (John 1:3).

Since *Jesus was with God* in the beginning, and since I'm realizing my life is *hidden in Christ* through whom all things were made, and since *God exists outside of time*, doesn't that mean that maybe, just maybe, somehow, *I was there in the beginning with God in a secret place*, like what is spoken of in Psalm 139?

Your deepest self, created in the secret place, never entered into slavery. Your deepest self never entered into exploitation. My deepest self, created by God - body, spirit and soul - would have never allowed the deceit that happened in June of 2001. That dark and dismal day, I withered away in secrecy with some kind of knowing that the boundary lines of my garden had been severely crossed.

My good friend Sarah once said to me, "The things that were done to you, the Lord did not ordain. He sees you as pure and spotless. His justice is white." And so I say to you, dear one, the things that were done to you, He did not ordain. He sees you, dear one, as pure and spotless.

I pray that out of His glorious riches he may strengthen you with power through his Spirit in your inner being. (Ephesians 3:16 NIV)

Malachi the Messenger

The name "Malachi" means *messenger*. Malachi was actually a prophet, one of the twelve minor prophets of the Old Testament, and the author of the book of Malachi. The book of Malachi foretells the coming of Christ, because Malachi was a prophet who received revelation of things to come. In scripture we learn, "Surely the Sovereign Lord does nothing without revealing his plan to his servants the prophets" (Amos 3:7 NIV).

Malachi also means *my messenger* or *my angel*. Malachi spoke of a prophet who would appear in the last days:

Behold I am going to send you Elijah the prophet before the coming of the great and terrible day of the Lord. (Malachi 4:5)

Malachi speaks of Elijah who was a prophet in the Old Testament, but because of the questions Jesus is asked by His disciples in the New Testament, we can gather that people likened John the Baptist to Elijah. John the Baptist was not Elijah, but he was acting like that predicted of Elijah in Malachi 4 by calling the people to repentance in anticipation of the coming day of the Lord, a day when God will visit His people for judgment and then blessing.

Those who move in the spirit of Elijah will also do as the prophet Elijah once did.

In 1 Kings 18:38, Elijah confronted the false prophets of Baal in a contest to determine who the true God was. Elijah actually brought into focus his own identity before the fire fell when he alluded to who, and Whose he was. Elijah built the altar (which represents the way we live our lives), and then, "Elijah replied to the captain of fifty, 'If I am a man of God, let fire come down from heaven and consume you and your fifty'" (2 Kings 1:10a).

Fire really did fall and consume the captain and those who followed him.

If there are actions made that are opposite of a new identity in Christ, the Lord will let us know, because that's what a good Father does - He brings correction. There is a distinction between what is righteous and what is wicked, and between what is right and what is wrong.

Where there are new altars of praise within the hearts of His sons and daughters, there is fire that burns away what is vile and idolatrous. The spirit of Elijah, by the Holy Spirit, is sent before the second coming of Jesus Christ. The spirit of Elijah causes honor between generations and to the Lord. Reconciliation is a byproduct of a new identity in Christ.

Reflections in a Mirror

We become what we behold.

God is justice and when we continue to look to Him, we act justly. When we learn who He is, we can learn who we are. In the past, I did not act in love, nor did I act justly. Learning to choose love and act rightly is an ongoing practice empowered through a relationship with God. Back then, what I looked at, what I *beheld*, didn't cause life. Once I learned Who I belonged to in light of Jesus Christ, I learned more of my identity.

Victory becomes a byproduct of the reality of an identity formed in Christ.

> For you are a holy people to the Lord your God; the Lord your God has chosen you to be a people for His own possession out of all the peoples who are on the face of the earth. (Deuteronomy 7:6)

> For now we see in a mirror dimly, but then face to face; now I know in part, but then I will know fully just as I also have been fully known. (1 Corinthians 13:12)

New names given by God in the Old Testament reflected a change in a person's life or character that God knew would take place. For instance, Jacob, which means *supplanter* (tries to take the place of or replace) was changed to Israel, which means *He strives with God*.

There are things you've been striving for. Like Israel, you have persisted, and through persistence comes an understanding of your true identity as a child of God. Some of the greatest miracles in life come out of seasons of strife, where God is teaching you who you really are.

Only God knows the identity of the children Corey and I desire to have after almost ten years of hoping and praying. The fingerprints I saw in the clouds spoke not only of the identity of the children we would have, but of the child I would have had.

God knows our deepest wounds, places of grief that only He can heal in His perfect timing. Only within the secret place of His presence is true healing and hope found.

In order for me to acknowledge the pain and find hope from past, I had to first learn about being a new creation in Christ. God knew that in order to address the grief in my heart that came with longing, there needed to be deeper rivers of life that came with knowledge of what Jesus did on the cross – what that meant for me, for her, and for the man who would have been the father.

IDENTITY KEY

1. What are you contending for in the realization of your identity as a child of God?

2. What scriptures support you as a new creation in Christ Jesus?

3. Who was Elijah and what did he do?

4. What is the meaning of your name which your parents or parent gave you?

5. Write down and speak out the scriptures found in this chapter which teach you about a new name God will give you.

WOMB

רֶחֶם

GRACE IN THE WOMB

GRACE KEY

He has made everything beautiful in its time. He has also set eternity in the human heart; yet no one can fathom what God has done from beginning to end.

Ecclesiastes 3:11 NIV

Beauty is in everything, in time.

In *The Secret Garden*, first published in 1911 by Frances Hodgson Burnett, Mary's uncle experienced grief that caused him to lock up the garden and throw away the key. In time, and after a dream of the one he longed for, he went back into the garden where beauty had once blossomed. For him, the garden was the place where his bride had tragically died. The grief he felt lingered for years, affecting everything and everyone around him. *In time* he experienced the joy of seeing his niece cultivate the garden back to life.

And it was there, in the garden, that he was able to reunite with his son whom he had pushed away for so long.

In Genesis, Joseph's dad Jacob also experienced the depths of grief when his sons told him the lie that their brother had died. Jacob refused to be comforted. Although scripture doesn't say this exactly, it's likely he suffered in grief until, *in time,* he came face-to-face with Joseph in Egypt.

It was likewise grief that hindered me from entering into the fullness of the garden of my life, even years into the restoration journey. The biggest thistle of all was death itself, which grew like poison ivy to pierce my soul with lies. Even though June 27th many years ago was the day that surrounded me in black, death would not have the final say. Little by little, I was able to acknowledge what happened as my heart softened in the light of love and forgiveness.

The Mississippi Letter

It was our first year of marriage.

I don't recall exactly how the letter had found its way into my hands, but it was meant for me to find. This letter is meant for many to read. Getting up in the night from where my husband and I laid together, I went to a room opposite from where we slept. As emotions welled up in my soul, I tried not to wake him at the sound of my crying. My heart felt like a teapot on a hot stove and the whistle sounded first in tears, then loud wails of grief as I thought of my baby.

At any time I could have a thought of her, but I always had to think of her in Heaven now.

As I read the letter, I heard what sounded like drums. It was an audible sound like a rhythm, a heartbeat, that synced up with mine. This was the very heartbeat of God, the Creator of my baby. Her heartbeat must have synced with His, and in that moment, as I began to read the letter, our hearts all synced together in a rhythm of sound.

The letter came from what was called the *Mississippi Mercy Journey*.

James Nesbit, a prophetic artist and musician, traveled with a team of prayer warriors, stopping at several sites along the Mississippi River. Many of the details of their journey have been recorded and made available on his website, but this is an excerpt from a letter of events that took place during one of their times of worship and declarations:

James, as he did at every site, shared the vision of *Mississippi Mercy*. On October 30, 2008 God gave him a vision of the 50 million babies that have been aborted in America. The babies were worshiping around the throne. God said to James, "The sound of their worship is unimaginable to you. A portion of their worshipful cry and part of their cry is mercy for their mommies and daddies and their grandparents who counseled their mothers to abort them." He said, "I love these innocents more than you know and I love their mommies and daddies and grandparents as well." God told him how He wanted to draw them unto Himself and heal them. God told James, "It is time that the worshipful sounds of the 50 million are released through America! As you, with understanding, position yourself between heaven and earth and ask for the floodgates of My mercy to be opened, in response to the cries of the eternals here, and your calling for My kingdom to manifest on earth, floodgates of mercy will be opened. When the floodgates of mercy are opened, everything changes!" God showed him how we are the lightning rods to release His eternal plans on the earth. He also showed him that this prayer journey, unlike the previous ones, was to start at the mouth of the river - the opening of the birth canal - and push up the river, against the flow and current course of this nation.

- From The Mississippi Letter

Life has a sound.

Healing and life both make a sound, and God knew I needed to experience both that night. That was the first night I told my husband about the abortion. Hearing his words that came with love, feeling his embrace, and knowing what I had read in the letter allowed me to finally be able to breathe again.

Ecclesiastes Promise

A dear friend of mine who has also experienced grief from abortion, has since been deeply impacted by God's love. The Lord has given her many comforting words as she has journeyed through healing, including finding comfort from a scripture verse out of the book of Ecclesiastes. She once told me that although it's difficult to find the beauty in the ashes of abortion, she knows that there is a promise to her: that He makes all things beautiful. Now, I too hold onto this promise, understanding that somehow God is making beauty from the tragedy and trauma of abortion.

In Ecclesiastes 3:11, we are told, "He has made everything beautiful in its time."

Everything means *everything.*

Battling the Deceiver with Truth

At the start of a new year, even years after reading the Mississippi Mercy letter, I had to choose grace over guilt. Instead of picking up my phone in the mornings, I was practicing picking up my Bible. While reading Exodus, the words jumped off the page and into my spirit. Even so, I was having a difficult time reading about the plagues and wrestling with some pestilence in my journey, so my prayer time became quite intense. As I answered each question in my devotional related to the scriptures, several thoughts surfaced.

One question in particular asked me to choose grace over guilt about something in my life. Condemning, snarling words brought torment: "You aborted your baby." Suddenly, I was having a flashback scene of being in that small room where my baby was taken from me. Guilt began to flood my soul as it often did at random and unexpected times when thoughts of my baby girl would come up. As my eyes flooded with tears, that feeling of grief surfaced. Again, I was working through grief in every one of its stages: denial, anger, bargaining, depression, and acceptance.

This time, I screamed out loud amidst my tears, "Yes! Yes, I did abort my baby." I actually agreed with the accuser, and then, something happened. I was reminded of what I had just read in Exodus about the blood over the doorpost that caused death to pass over the Israelites.

Another scene of being in that room flashed in my mind.

Holy Spirit whispered, "*I was there.*" The ultrasound photo that was taken showing life in my womb was also shown as a picture in my spirit.

Again, I heard a whisper, "*Your baby is with me.*"

A new picture was given, replacing the old one of that sterile, dark place. Holy Spirit flooded my thoughts with scriptures about being a new creation in Christ. He reminded me of the blood of Jesus Christ and that His blood has the power to atone (*redeem, repair, reconcile*). Because of love, "... in Christ Jesus you who formerly were far off have been brought near by the blood of Christ" (Ephesians 2:13).

Death had come to take my baby that day in June, but there was more to the story.

Death was overcome.

I remembered the Mississippi Letter and began to thank God for His life, for sending His Son Jesus, who overcame death to give hope and life.

Life is now hidden in Christ - both hers and mine. I hear the Lord whisper:

Trinity connects your womb with your baby, your baby is with Me, your Father. Receive healing in this truth, in Jesus Christ. Jesus is healing. He is the very essence of life and healing and His cleansing blood runs through your veins. This blood is the same life-giving blood that was and is shared with the life of your baby. You are more connected than you could ever know and you will see her face.

The Tabernacle in the Womb

The book of Leviticus gives us a picture of a tabernacle.

God can be quite particular as to how to construct a dwelling or sanctuary. He gave specific instructions as to what the tabernacle was supposed to look like, from colors to types of materials, and even the exact measurements and ways of doing things so that the people of Israel would be safe. The tabernacle (*residence, dwelling place*) was the portable, earthly place where God met with the children of Israel from the time of the exodus from Egypt through the conquering of the land.

The womb is another type of secret place, a place of safety and protection that was created to bring nourishment. From the very formations of being woven together in the secret place of the womb, there is a deep-seated instinct, a natural desire for safety and nourishment. When a child is within the mother's womb, the umbilical cord, also called the *navel string*, is a conduit between the developing embryo or fetus and the placenta. I've often thought of prayer as a lifeline like this.

During prenatal development, the umbilical cord is physiologically and genetically part of the fetus and contains two arteries and one vein, the umbilical vein. The umbilical vein supplies the baby fetus with nutrient-rich blood from the placenta. Conversely, the fetal heart pumps nutrient-depleted blood through the umbilical arteries back to the placenta. What a beautiful picture of blood and oxygen being shared between mother and baby. To take this a step further the following information from Sarah Terzo with LiveAction highlights the beauty of a baby's heartbeat:

"Science teaches without reservation that life begins at fertilization (conception). It is a scientific fact that an organism exists after fertilization that did not exist before. This new organism has its own DNA distinct from the mother and father, meaning that it is a unique person. As the embryo grows, it develops a heartbeat (22 days after fertilization), its own circulatory system, and its own organs. From fertilization, it is a new organism that is alive and will continue to grow and develop as long as nutrition is provided and its life is not ended through violence or illness." [2]

One single cell, which results from the fertilization of the female egg cell by the male sperm cell, carries life. The cell (from the Latin word "cella," meaning *small room*) is the basic structural, functional, and biological unit of all living things. In other words, a cell is considered a basic unit of life. Clearly, according to modern molecular biology, life is present from the moment of conception.

To put this all together, the body is a temple for the Holy Spirit, a dwelling place. The womb is to be a safe place that provides protection and nutrients to a growing human life who is enclosed within walls, almost like a tabernacle or temple. Within a life-giving source such as the womb, oxygen and blood are shared.

In my teenage years, I did not understand the value of life, neither my own nor the baby that I carried at that time. It was not only myself who was deceived that day, but also the person who took me to have the abortion.

Speak Up, Do Not Be Silent

A mistake some churches are making regarding abortion is rightly sensing its destructive influence, but then remaining silent to spare those who are hurting. I once asked a pastor why he had never preached on the value of life and the lies of abortion. There were several women in the congregation who had been deceived into having an abortion, and most of them were suffering in silence.

Instead of him preaching a message, he allowed me to share my testimony along with a word of grace, mercy, and forgiveness. I also spoke on the realities of abortion and the significance of protecting life. There was no condemnation in the message. After the service, several women were not only able to share their stories, but there was time for healthy grieving and prayer together.

Many of us would benefit from allowing times of grieving with our sisters.

One of the ways I was able to experience deeper restoration was by talking and listening to Jenna, the dear friend who taught me about the Ecclesiastes promise. In her past, Jenna had also been deceived into having an abortion. Now, as a Spirit-filled believer who loves God and allows His leading in her life, Jenna has found healing in the depths of the Father's love. If not for our conversations, I would have struggled to find anything beautiful out the ashes of lies and deceit. Together, we have prayed, talked and cried. We have also prayed for the many women who are suffering in silence from the wounds of abortion.

Godly sorrow is cleansing. Tears wash away the ashes.

Godly sorrow will heal hearts that have been suffering. Speaking up and speaking out in the right places, and with the right people, will also cause healing because silence can be destructive. We overcome by the word of our testimony, and the blood of the lamb (see Revelation 12:11).

Several years ago, before I left a counseling job at a major health facility, I was approached by a young woman who told me that because I shared the reality of abortion with her, she decided to have her baby instead of going through with terminating the life in her womb. Today, she has a beautiful baby girl and she is a fantastic, brave mother. Stories like this one must be told, even in the places where we are told not to speak up or speak out.

Let's Talk About Best Health

The pro-choice movement talks about "best health," and giving "healthy options" for women, yet, the greatest pain in my life that was described as an "option," was associated with abortion. Death is a destructive and deceitful "option." The option of death causes grief, and grief causes sickness.

The pain, grief and physical damage that comes from abortion is traumatic and unhealthy. After life had been taken from my womb, I was put into a small room. Alone in that room, the walls seemed to cave in on me. For days I felt physical pain. In the depths of my inner self, I knew that what had just happened was wrong. It was the feeling of being alone that would stay with me until I encountered Jesus in very real and tangible ways many years later. Before that, I hardened my heart because it hurt too much to even think about.

To love God is to love and value life:

> For with You is the fountain of life, in Your light we see light. (Psalm 36:9)
> God is the Giver of Life. (see Acts 17:25)
> God is the Author of Life. (see Acts 3:15)
> God is the Defender of Life. (see Psalm 27:1)
> God is the Restorer of Life. (see Ruth 4:15)

To choose best health is to honor body, spirit and soul - both our own, and if pregnant, the body, spirit and soul of that baby who is being formed in the safe place of the womb. Healthy, honoring, Spirit-filled self would never authorize the death of one's own child.

Pro-life is pro-women's health.

Pro-women's health is pro-life.

Grace and Mercy

Grace is *God's unmerited favor*. In the Bible, grace and mercy are often paired together. Mercy is God withholding judgment; grace is

God giving me blessing or good that I do not deserve. Because of God's mercy, I do not receive the judgment of God against my sins. Because of God's grace, I receive eternal life and a promise, like the promise in Ecclesiastes.

Jesus Christ is both grace and mercy. Grace meets us where we are, but does not leave us where we are found.

> My grace is sufficient for you, for power is perfected in weakness. Most gladly, therefore, I will rather boast about my weaknesses, so that the power of Christ may dwell in me. (2 Corinthians 12:9)

The Hebrew word for grace is "chen" which means *adornment, charm, charming, favor, grace*. Because of the greatest act of love, God is speaking grace, mercy and favor over you, and over me. Each of our storylines are woven with grace.

The damage of a child's death is so dark and severe that we often cannot see the full picture because of the tragedy itself. While I cannot determine the origination of the following quote, reading it will help us to understand the Ecclesiastes promise just a little bit more:

> "It may take a lifetime to understand that within that dark and ugly place there was beauty and love so strong that not even death could dishevel it. In fact, the beauty that is love continues even after and through death and the impact of that trauma brings us closer to the love that we shared for that person and all the ways love of that individual has affected our lives and the lives of others. The secondary beauty that has an everlasting ripple effect on other people's lives and through eternity is what living is truly about. All about the quality and not so much the quantity. When we can see love where darkness used to reside, we can finally turn our lives, and those around us, into something glorious."

— AUTHOR UNKNOWN

It is unbearable to think of what happened - that my baby was taken from the womb, the very place that was meant to provide safety and bring nourishment - unless I look through the lens of the cross and the life of Jesus Christ. Only there, in Christ, do I find grace and mercy.

Somehow tragedy is turning into a *love story* that will not fully be understood until coming face-to-face with Jesus.

He knew each of our storylines before we were knitted together in the womb. If you, like so many of us, were once deceived by the lies of abortion, please know the story isn't over. There are bowls in Heaven filled with the tears and the prayers of those who've longed for a different story other than what the lies of abortion spoke.

Not one tear is unaccounted for.

Not one prayer has gone unheard.

The memories I have of that dark day in June and the deep grief that influenced and affected everything have since been replaced with song, sights of healing, and hope for a different story. Now I have visions of my daughter in the throne room and I am beginning to hear the sound of her song.

In the fall of 2018, moments before falling asleep, she came to mind with substance of depth and reality. With tears in my eyes, my stomach in knots and my head in a daze of searching, pain echoed within. In that dark moment, light broke through with truth. I saw a picture of a vase.

Holy Spirit reminded me that I was that clay, and He, the Potter.

But now, O Lord, You are our Father, we are the clay, and You our potter; And all of us are the work of Your hand. (Isaiah 64:8)

His presence permeated all of me - body, spirit and soul - until I experienced oneness with Him that came with peace instead of torment. Within that moment, I was able to breathe again. As I was reminded of her, I saw a pink rose in that vase. This picture indicated her life within the clay, within that space of oneness, within Christ alone.

A rose in a vase.

A life within a life.

From the beginning, there is a love song that God has written. This love song heals broken hearts and broken bodies, and brings redemption to longing. The love song sings of hope and forgiveness and it echoes with sounds of grace.

As my husband and I have moved forward in the adoption process, ten years into our marriage, I've been continually reminded of grace. Grace is a beautiful thing. Grace is a song. Grace is the unmerited favor, the kindness of God we do not deserve.

Grace is also the name of a little girl who would be 18 years old. Grace is the little girl on the front cover of Volume 1 of *The Garden Keys*, inside the garden walls. I think of her every day. Every single day. There are moments when tears rage forth that bleed with longing. Would she have been a writer, a dancer, or an artist?

God has created a love song that I've only begun to learn. He can take the darkest plans of evil's intent and turn it around for the one who has been called according to His purpose. He has given me faith to believe I have been called according to His good purposes, because of this new life I've found in Jesus Christ. This is grace.

With glimpses of her in His presence, singing songs of redemption that I am beginning to hear, I know that someday our love stories will meet within the perfect chord.

It was the option presented to me, my "right," my "choice" and one which was heavily influenced. It was the lie that coerced its grip not only on me, but also unto the one who took me to Planned Parenthood where this destructive, traumatizing choice was carried out. This was no plan for parenting. This was no good plan for health.

Abortion is a lie that has been whispered into the ears of a culture as an option, a woman's right. This option brings damage to a woman's health and her long-term emotional well being. This I know for certain, abortion is trauma.

Only God's love, light, and truth can bring some kind of healing.

The morning after my encounter with hope, I was sent a picture from a friend, also an artist, who lives in Switzerland. With thoughts of a painting for me, the image she couldn't get out of her mind was a rose within a vase, a life within a life.

She drew the picture, led by Holy Spirit, in about the same time frame I was crying out with longing for the daughter I know is in the Father's arms. A life within a life, the picture given to me by my Abba, Adonai, who gives life, hope and a new story for His glory.

There is a love song within this story.

There is hope for what's to come. Until then, and at the very moment when I see her face-to-face, when God the Father is worshiped, I am joining in the song of the eternals. When you worship King Jesus, you are joining in with the song of the eternals.

These songs unite Heaven and Earth.

I hear the Lord saying to His bride, to His daughters and to His sons:

With Me, your child is with Me, a part of Me and I am in you,
and you are in Me. We are one with the Father. Find life in Me.
Your child is My child.

He has made everything beautiful, *in time.*

GRACE KEY

1. Invite the Holy Spirit and love of the Father into any places of sadness or grief.

2. Speak out loud the scripture declarations found in this chapter. Write the scriptures in your journal.

3. If you're experiencing grief at the loss of a loved one, write a letter exactly expressing your thoughts and hopes. Allow yourself to experience the emotions as they come.

4. If you've had an abortion, choose forgiveness if there was anyone else involved. Pray for the man who would have been the father. *Remember, forgiveness doesn't make right what happened, but it does allow you to heal.*

5. If you've had an abortion and you haven't already, consider naming your baby.

6. What can you choose grace over guilt about?

4

AMYGDALA AND SING

SING KEY

And she will sing there as in the days of her youth, As in the day when she came up from the land of Egypt.

Hosea 2:15b

Moving about my grandparents' house as a little girl, I would carry a piece of crystal that resembled a microphone. Making sure no one heard or saw me, I would sing into this pretend microphone. Sometimes, if I really knew the coast was clear, I would dance as well. Moments of singing and dancing made me feel alive and free.

The crystal microphone was a piece of my grandma and grandpa's dining set, which was only taken out for special occasions. In my eyes, it was always a special occasion to sing.

King David, the psalmist, skilled musician and war hero, often retreated to a secret place where he would play an instrument to worship. Whether he was returning home from battle as a victor or running from an enemy and fleeing for his life, music was soothing and comforting. He knew music released something sweet, which was the power of song and its effect on his body, spirit, and soul. In essence, his goal was not to heal, but to worship God. In that place of worshiping God, he found healing.

Amygdala in the Brain

Science has been hard at work trying to explain why singing has such a calming, yet energizing effect on people. What researchers are beginning to discover is that singing is like an infusion of the perfect tranquilizer, the kind that both soothes your nerves and elevates the happy chemicals in your brain. The surge of calm that comes from singing comes from endorphins, a hormone which is associated with feelings of pleasure.

The amygdala, an almond-shaped mass of cells located deep within the temporal lobes of your brain, is a part of the limbic system structure that is involved in your emotions and motivations, particularly those that are related to survival.

For example, the processing of emotions such as fear, anger and pleasure are all a part of the amygdala. The amygdala is also responsible for determining what memories are stored and where they are kept in the brain. It is thought that this determination is based on the size of the emotional response an event evokes.

The first time I heard a teaching on the amygdala, I was at Exodus Cry's Abolition Summit. This was a powerful time of equipping for anyone involved in the abolition movement to bring an end to commercial sexual exploitation, which includes human sex trafficking.

At the summit, Dr. Dan Allender presented on the power of singing related to its effects on the amygdala and in healing trauma. Describing the relationship between singing and the amygdala he said:

"We need to understand that when you've been traumatized your brain changes. A portion of your limbic system called the hippocampus shrinks somewhere up to 8-12 percent, and that part of our brain regulates emotions. There is a portion of your brain affected by trauma called the amygdala. It's an interplay between the amygdala and the hippocampus and the amygdala. The amygdala is constantly looking for danger and warning the brain that there is trouble. The hippocampus is actually going, 'No, you're okay. These are wires. They are necessary for music and for speech. You are well.' All the while you thought they were snakes. Remember, the hippocampus shrinks as a result of trauma. Thank God the hippocampus can grow to the degree we begin to tell our stories in a way in which we can regulate our own bodies' struggle. Here's the sweet piece of news: when you sing and hear music, your amygdala dances. Your brain changes when you sing, when you hear music, when you worship, *when you have a chance to be in the presence of beauty, your body begins to change.*

"If you are involved in addressing victims of sexual abuse, they need movement. They literally need to dance. They literally need to have their bodies return to them by an acknowledgment of the fact that we are sinews, muscles. We are bones and movement. What evil wishes to do through the experience of betrayal is to turn you against your body and through powerlessness to take away your effectiveness in this world and ultimately to bring shame to your body." [3]

Dr. Allender spoke of trauma including sexual abuse, exploitation, and sex trafficking. I would add, trauma from addiction and the lifestyle that so unpleasantly accompanies such, as well as the effects of abortion, can also be included in what is considered as trauma. But, beauty can bring a different story.

Beauty mesmerizes us.

We are like our Creator, made in His image, and so we are attracted to beauty. We can love wildly and move without restraint in a dance of freedom. Purpose is found in relationship to Christ, and then, through the entrance of doing what we love. Sometimes we discover who we are in Christ by doing what we love. There is a hunger in the human heart to create, whether it be through song, dance, the arts, building, or designing.

Endorphins, the pleasure hormone, along with oxytocin, another hormone released during singing, have been found to alleviate anxiety and stress. Oxytocin also enhances feelings of trust and bonding, which may explain why still more studies have found that singing lessens feelings of depression and loneliness.

Singing can literally help move us from fear to freedom, from sickness to healing. Singing the Word of God, in the freedom of Holy Spirit-given words are some of my most cherished times with God.

Gates of Pearl

In Revelation 21:21 we read, "And the twelve gates were twelve pearls; each one of the gates was a single pearl. And the street of the city was pure gold, like transparent glass." It's interesting that the gates are made of a single pearl. God could have made the gates using any other material or gem, but it was a pearl that He chose. While it's true that many gems are caused from friction, pearls are literally created by irritation.

While on a trip to India, shortly after Corey and I were married, I experienced a significant amount of fear after finding out my wallet had been stolen. Feeling overwhelmed with concerns of how I was going to get home, the only thing I could think of was getting alone with God, *"Enter into the gates with thanksgiving and praise!"*

Leaving the commotion of people talking and the police grilling me with questions in an attempt to help, I got up and went into a different room. With the door shut behind me, I dropped to my knees and began to thank God for various things. I was trying to remind myself how faithful He had been. I began to sing, not caring if anyone heard me. With tears streaming down my face, I did what I had learned to do, sing and worship God.

While singing and thanking God, Holy Spirit led me to make a few declarations. From my seated position in the throne room, I declared that the stealing spirit connected to the disappearance of my wallet would indeed return it. I'm not sure exactly what was said, but it came from somewhere deep inside. Sometimes, in the church, we get too hung up on saying something the right way. I just told that deceiving spirit it needed to return my wallet and that it had no authority.

That day I felt a mixture of emotions. It was the wedding day of my now brother and sister-in-law, who are dear to me. The wedding was beautiful. However, I was so shook up from what had happened that I didn't play music there in the streets of India as I was supposed to.

Looking back, I see how that deceiving spirit sought to distract me so that I would not play ministering music in a place of heavy Hinduism. Maybe the deceit of the enemy was to distract and silence the music and voice of a Spirit-filled daughter. After all, his tactics are to seduce, sedate and then silence. Perhaps this has been his plan all along, to silence the sons and daughters of God.

Late that night, after the wedding, Corey and I were nestled into our little room covered with scripture verses when we heard a knock on the door.

At the door was our friend from the home where my wallet had been stolen. All he said was, "Who do you trust?" Puzzled at his question, and in a daze of exhaustion, I said, "Corey."

Holding up my wallet he proceeded to say, "It is God who you trust."

Someone had thrown my wallet back through the gates of the house where it had been stolen. This was also the same place where I sang out loud to worship King Jesus.

Enter into the gates with thanksgiving and praise!

Narrow Way

To act in truth, which causes healing, there is a necessary

process of growing up into maturity. Jesus tells us in Matthew that we are supposed to, "Enter through the narrow gate; for the gate is wide and the way is broad that leads to destruction, and there are many who enter through it" (Matthew 7:13). Furthermore, in the book of John He states, "I am the gate; whoever enters through me will be saved. They will come in and go out, and find pasture" (John 10:9 NIV).

When we act in obedience to what is moral, we are entering in that narrow way. To know morality, we must know truth, and to know truth, we must look to Jesus Christ. Don't let anyone ever tell you that because you are saved by grace, you can act however you want. As my good friend Albert used to say, "That's hogwash!" Living out the Christian life can be hard work because it is opposite of the world's way, but it leads to life, shalom peace and complete restoration.

When it's difficult, sing anyway. When it doesn't make sense, give thanks. When you stand for what is moral you are entering in through the narrow gate.

Experiential Living Tabernacle

Synesthesia takes place where a certain tone or wave of sound produces a color. A note is played and a color is seen. This isn't crazy, this is Holy Spirit and this is how things happen in the Kingdom of Heaven. In some of the most incredible times of worship, I've seen colors paired with certain tones. When reality is experienced in Spirit-led worship, the senses can literally mix.

While in Washington DC at Revolution 2018, James Nesbit and a group of radicals for Jesus worshiped in spirit and in truth. They led some of the most anointed worship I've been a part of corporately. As declarations about the Seven Spirits of God (see Revelation 1:4) were released, I began to smell the most amazing scent that reminded me of evergreen trees, as did others around me, including my husband. The Lord brought to mind a scripture from Hosea: "His shoots will sprout, and his beauty will be like the olive tree and his fragrance like the cedars of Lebanon" (Hosea 14:6). We were literally smelling the fragrance of Christ. Along with the fragrance came an unexplainable reality that God was in our midst and we were in His.

In this season there are new sounds being released from Heaven that have created a tone of blue. Blue mixes with green. New sounds are rushing into the hearts of the sons and daughters of God as they press into times of worship. Blue is a color that represents Holy Spirit. Blue is also the color for a priestly garment and some of the articles that were in the tabernacle.

In the Old Testament, the portable tabernacle contained a courtyard, and was built according to God's perfect instructions given to Moses. The tabernacle was the place where the presence of the Lord would descend to meet with Moses and the priests (see Exodus 40:33-35).

It took skilled musicians, creators, and the perfect design to build the tabernacle. Certain objects like the altar of incense and colors such as blue, bronze, and scarlet were all important parts of the tabernacle.

Millions of people could not fit into the tent of meeting that was set up. Therefore, in the Hebrew culture of the past, what was given to them was their own private sanctuary, their own tent. Each tent was like a secret fortress where they could meet with God.

Each person had their own tent.

Each person sang in their own tent.

The Jewish prayer shawl is called a *tallit*. A prayer room tallit contains two Hebrew words: "tal" meaning *tent* and "it" meaning *little*. Thus, when you have a tallit, you have little tent. The Jewish people pull the little shawl up over their heads, forming a tent, where they begin to chant, sing Hebrew psalms, and call upon God. It is an intimate, private, and set apart time totally focused on God.

Jesus told His disciples that, "...when He, the Spirit of Truth, comes, He will guide you into all truth" (see John 16:13). He reveals to our minds the whole counsel of God as it relates to worship, doctrine, and doing the right things. Time alone with the Lord, or in a group of Spirit-filled friends, while singing or dancing, can be an intimate, private and set-apart time to focus on God.

> Or do you not know that your body is a temple of the Holy Spirit who is in you, whom you have from God, and that you are not your own? For you have been bought with a price: therefore glorify God in your body. (1 Corinthians 6:19-20)

Not only are our bodies a temple, but we are seated in Christ and being built up by God Himself. In Corinthians the Apostle Paul put it this way:

> Or what agreement has the temple of God with idols? For we are the temple of the living God; just as God said, "I will dwell in them and walk among them; and I will be their God, and they shall be My people. Therefore, come out from their midst and be separate," says the Lord. "And do not touch what is unclean; And I will welcome you. And I will be a father to you, and you shall be sons and daughters to Me," says the Lord Almighty. (2 Corinthians 6:16-18)

Singing Deborah

Deborah was a prophet, judge, counselor, warrior and the wife of Lapidoth, according to Judges 4-5. Deborah did more than prophesy, she roused the nation from its lethargy and despair. Hers was a fearless and unsolicited devotion to the freedom of God's people. Empowered by God, she caused awakening that empowered the people to free themselves from their wretched captivity.

Deborah sang and shouted, "Awake! Awake!" We too must sing in our own tents, "Awake! Awake!" to rouse ourselves and the daughters to morality, justice and love. There is a war cry sound and song that is erupting from the womb of many daughters who were once exploited and deceived. These are the many daughters who are being awakened to God's love and forgiveness as they prepare for the greatest song and dance that will cause them to come through the narrow way.

When I think of the narrow place, I think about the aisle that the bride walks down before she gets married. In order for the wedding to take place, the bride must not only respond to the invitation, but she must get ready.

In an awakening, there are seasons of waiting that are necessary to embrace.

SING KEY

1. What did you learn about singing and its relationship to healing from trauma?

2. What scripture verses can you find about singing? Write them down in your journal.

3. What is the tabernacle?

4. Who was Deborah and what did she do?

5. Write about a time you gave thanks or praised God even when it was challenging to do so.

WAITING LIKE HANNAH

WAITING KEY

When will it be Spring?

Mary Lennox

In "The Secret Garden," Mary waited for roses to grab the walls of the garden like a veil. In Genesis, Joseph waited to see his father after many years of living in Egypt. In his waiting, it's likely there were times he wondered if he would ever see his father again. My husband and I have waited more than a decade for children of our own. I will be waiting even longer until the day I see the face of my daughter Grace.

In the Old Testament we learn about Hannah, referred to as a "mother of Israel," who had long hoped for a baby. In her season of waiting, a time marked with anticipation, she held onto a promise, not knowing that God was working something deep within her.

In the pain of waiting, there is beauty.

The season of waiting and long-suffering was necessary to bring about the outcome. Hannah would be a mother to the last judge of Israel. By God's perfect design, it would be her son who would appoint Israel's first king. Hannah was one of Elkanah's two wives. Elkanah's other wife, and mother of several of his children, unmercifully taunted the childless Hannah.

Imagine what it must have been like for Hannah.

The emotions and thoughts that flooded her mind from the never-ending taunting as well as the strong desire to have a baby caused an intense response. Under pressure she held onto promise. Hannah had to hold onto faith, which is "...the substance of things hoped for, the evidence of things not seen" (Hebrews 11:1 NKJV).

Elkanah did his best to console her and confirm his love for her, but Hannah would not be consoled. She prayed fervently for a son. Finally, she made a vow that if the Lord would bless her with a son, she would dedicate him to the Lord's service. This was a Spirit-led moment which God had ordained. The Lord's plan called for faith, dedication and perseverance *in the waiting*. Within a year, Samuel was born to Elkanah and Hannah. Indeed, Samuel was a mighty prophet at a pivotal time in Israel's history.

Samuel appointed the first two kings of Israel, Saul and David. He also judged Israel, restored law and order, and began regular religious worship in the land (see 1 Samuel 4:15-18; 7:3-17). You could say the timing of his entrance into the world was one of great significance.

Hannah had patiently waited for years, praying persistently for what she hoped for, a baby. She knew long-suffering. During those years, she never gave up or believed lies about herself or God. Being rooted and grounded in the Word, the goodness of God, and the truth of identity as a child of God makes the waiting worth the outcome of promise.

Samuel was born in answer to his mother's prayers.

Hannah remembered God with gratitude. Her joy was enriched because Samuel was the product of the Lord's power. She spoke boldly in the midst of those who would ridicule her and was not ashamed because the Lord was the God of her salvation. Hannah's prayer is one of celebrating and honoring God:

> Then Hannah prayed and said,
>
> "My heart exults in the Lord; My horn is exalted in the Lord, my mouth speaks boldly against my enemies, because I rejoice in Your salvation. There is no one holy like the Lord, indeed, there is no one besides You, nor is there any rock like our God. Boast no more so very proudly, do not let arrogance come out of your mouth; For the Lord is a God of knowledge, and with Him actions are weighed. The bows of the mighty are shattered, but the feeble gird on strength. Those who were full hire themselves out for bread, but those who were hungry cease to hunger. Even the barren gives birth to seven, but she who has many children languishes. The Lord kills and makes alive; He brings down to Sheol and raises up. The Lord makes poor and rich; He brings low, He also exalts. He raises the poor from the dust, He lifts the needy from the ash heap to make them sit with nobles, and inherit a seat of honor; For the pillars of the earth are the Lord's, and He set the world on them. He keeps the feet of His godly ones, but the wicked ones are silenced in darkness; For not by might shall a man prevail. Those who contend with the Lord will be shattered; Against them He will thunder in the heavens, the Lord will judge the ends of the earth; And He will give strength to His king, And will exalt the horn of His anointed." (1 Samuel 2:1-10)

Hannah's prayer is one of depth that radiates with gratitude and acknowledgment of God. In her waiting, she persisted. There are others who have waited for their hope, their dream of destiny like a promise to manifest, as did Hannah. Persevering faith that wrestles for a blessing displays the kind of heart that God is after. The greatest gifts are not meant to be given to the faint of heart who do not pursue God.

Rachel, Joseph's mother, cried out, "Give me children, or else I die!" Rachel had both Benjamin and Joseph, and it was Joseph the dreamer who was elevated in success in the Egyptian government. It was also Joseph who saved his entire family from starvation during the time of drought.

Author Corey Russell captures the concept of waiting before he lists principles of intercession in his book *Prayer, Why Our Words to God Matter*. In his examples of those who waited in a season of barrenness he writes:

> In the New Testament, Elizabeth was barren until God supernaturally opened her womb. John the Baptist broke four centuries of prophetic silence over the nation, and Jesus called him the greatest man ever born of a woman (Mathew 11:11). Why is this? It takes the cry of the barren to birth the prophetic. God needs Hannahs to give birth to Samuels - people willing to walk the long and lonely road of the wilderness in order to see God's greatness manifest. God doesn't want our religious prayers. He desires the deepest parts of us; He only wants a groan to arise that reveals and purifies our heart. Only after we have been stripped and entered into complete desperation and dependence can we be trusted with the promise. In Isaiah 54 the prophet declares, "Sing O barren, you who have not borne!... For more are the children of the desolate than the children of the married woman" (Isaiah 54:1). The pain of barrenness and the reality of crying out prepare to carry the weight of the more. [4]

Be Still and Know

Hannah took time to pray and ask, and a cry rose up from within her. Her deep cried out to God's deep. She gave thanks and worshiped. Rachel waited in a season where she didn't have children, and yet, she turned to God and trusted Him in the process.

The goodness of waiting and being still as we seek God creates trust in Him and His perfect plan. In Psalm 46:10 we are told to be still and know that He is God. In other words, don't worry, look to God, and trust in His timing.

Waiting shaped Hannah's faith, just as waiting will shape your faith as well as my own. In the waiting, the question is: *Do you trust in God's good plan?*

> Be still before the Lord and wait patiently for Him. (Psalm 37:7a NIV)

Long Suffering

For many of us, waiting has been like suffering for a long time. Keeping thoughts and emotions in check can be a challenge in the season when expectations are carried. In the midst of waiting, there is a miracle in the making. It has taken me a journey through Egypt and almost 12 years of sober recovery to actually learn what long-suffering means. I need to actually *practice* it daily in this season of my life. Long-suffering is fruit of the Spirit.

We can take comfort in knowing that Jesus understands what it is like to wait. He knows what it means to long for something. Being with His beloved bride is what He yearns for. The longing of waiting for what one hopes for causes character to be revealed.

> And not only this, but we also exult in our tribulations, knowing that tribulation brings about perseverance; and perseverance, proven character; and proven character, hope; and hope does not disappoint, because the love of God has been poured out within our hearts through the Holy Spirit who was given to us. (Romans 5:3-5)

Hannah means *grace* and *favor*. Although Hannah was barren for a season, it was for purpose. There was favor upon her life. Like Jacob wrestled for a blessing, so too did Hannah. In her barrenness, she cried out to God, contending for a blessing. A blessing was birthed.

What have you been praying and longing for?

Through the midst of the numerous questions and suggestions made by friends as to our desire for children, I've trusted God's plan. Waiting is a key. Listening and being still in the waiting, is a part of that key. There was a season where I battled significantly, and yet through that time, I learned more about God's love, healing, and forgiveness.

After ten years of praying for children of our own, I know now that I needed to detox from Babylon before raising up children to love and honor God, themselves, and others. There has continued to be a deep healing that has needed to take place. At the perfect time, I know we will have children of our own.

Waiting comes with refinement.

There is hope for children after the deceit of abortion. Many who have had an abortion are now blessed with children. As we wait and pray for children, the longing in my heart to someday unite with Grace sings loudly. Coupled with the desire to unite with Grace is the longing to see Jesus face-to-face.

That day of seeing Jesus face-to-face will come for all of us.

May we, like Hannah, demonstrate the same faith, exultation, trust, and hope during times of waiting and in times of rejoicing when the promise has finally come about.

WAITING KEY

1. What are some things in Hannah's prayer that stick out to you?

2. What is something or someone you have waited for? How did you handle the longing?

3. Write in your journal and then speak out loud five different scripture verses that have to do with patience, long-suffering and/or waiting.

4. Ecclesiastes 5:1 says:

> "Guard your steps as you go to the house of God and draw near to listen rather than to offer the sacrifice of fools; for they do not know they are doing evil."

Start with just a few minutes, then increase that time to 10 minutes of simply being still and listening to God, instead of talking. Close your eyes, keep a focus on your breath, but keep in mind you are going near God to listen. Waiting means learning to listen.

6

SIGNS AND SYMBOLS

SIGNS AND SYMBOLS KEY

It is the glory of God to conceal a matter, but the glory of kings is to search out a matter.

Proverbs 25:2

After a long, dangerous journey, the three wise men met destiny face-to-face. The wise men had not only studied the prophecies that were meant to be a sign, but they studied the stars in the night sky, which drew their attention to the birth of the Messiah.

Signs are meant to point to something, or to bring attention and raise awareness. Symbols represent. The word "sign" is translated from the Greek word *semeion,* which is used in a passage in Luke: "This will be a sign for you: you will find a baby wrapped in cloths and lying in a manger" (Luke 2:12). The angel made it clear to the shepherds that when they would see the sign of a baby wrapped in cloths in a manger, they would in fact be seeing the Savior.

There are signs and symbols of significance that your Creator would like to draw your attention to. No sign or symbol is to be worshiped. We do not fall into the trap of demanding signs or symbols on account of unbelief. Jesus never fell into the trap of people, or especially Satan who demanded Jesus prove Himself with a sign or a miracle. Jesus didn't have to prove anything to those who sought to manipulate. But He did, and does, give signs to those who seek Him.

As you read this chapter, "I pray that the eyes of your heart may be enlightened, so that you will know what is the hope of His calling, what are the riches of the glory of His inheritance in the saints" (Ephesians 1:18).

An Awakening to Get Our Attention

Through the years of my own continued restoration journey, my God, Elohim, has used His creation, numbers, and even colors to get my attention. This is what happens in an awakening. The signs, symbols, cycles and seasons of God belong to God. He desires for us to understand His timetable and He wants us to listen when His creation speaks. Over the last several years especially, awakening through nature has increased exponentially. We're in a time when the land itself is crying out for righteousness and justice.

The title *El* means "powerful, strength and might." Elohim, in His great power, moves by His Spirit to speak to His children in such awesome ways. In Genesis 1:14 God said, "Let there be lights in the expanse of the heavens to separate the day from the night. And let them be for signs and seasons and for days and years." On the fourth day of God's work, He created the lights, the sun, the moon and the stars. In this scripture the word *seasons* means "appointed times."

Some of these signs and symbols may have caught your attention since you were a young child. I've always loved gazing at the stars. Looking at the stars makes me feel a kind of connection with others throughout all of time. The stars that Hannah and Deborah looked at are the same stars I can see. Stars symbolize that light can shine in the dark.

For my husband, a symbol of his youth was a hatchet. That hatchet was a token of hard work. The chopped up piles of wood showed character that demonstrated a hard working young man.

Like many of us, my husband also went through seasons of stumbling through Egypt. Eventually, he was led out of the captivity of alcohol use, and into the promised land of freedom through sobriety. The symbol of Corey's youth has remained the same. Even though there were tough times, that hatchet represented a hard working man who has built a relationship with God, a life of sobriety, a business of his own and a ministry we are able to serve in together.

For myself, the crystal imitation microphone from my youth has been a symbol for singing. And since singing brings healing, this particular sign and symbol also represents freedom and restoration.

People are fascinated with signs and symbols. Living in God's creation as sons and daughters who were originally given authority to have dominion, a symbol in nature or a sign in numbers can be a visible sign of something invisible.

Signs and symbols are all around us.

For example, the lion is a symbol of courage and the eagle is a symbol of protection. In Psalms 91 we are told He will cover us with His pinions, and under His wings we find refuge. The eagle also represents focus, as sight is the strongest of the eagle's senses. The eagle's vision is four to five times better than that of a human. And the fact that eagles are monogamous means they mate for life, which is pretty amazing.

If God wants to get our attention, He can open up the mouth of a donkey: "The Lord opened the mouth of the donkey, and she said to Balaam, 'What have I done to you, that you have struck me these three times?'" (Numbers 22:28). Now, I can't say I've ever heard an animal talk, but I have heard the sounds of choirs of angels singing. While Holy Spirit whispers within, there have also been times when I've either heard the audible voice of God or the voice of the Angel of the Lord. Such instances happened throughout the scriptures and they are happening now.

If there is repetition of certain signs or symbols that are being highlighted to you, it's likely there is a message. Think about it. Have you ever seen certain number patterns over and over again, or perhaps experienced the continuation of the same dream? There is a great awakening to the senses to experience God in these times. The entrance into the garden has everything to do with an awakening. In the spring when flowers finally bloom, our senses are awakened to color, sight and the sounds of the season.

Numbers and Hebrew Letters

We can learn a lot about the meaning of numbers by reading and studying scripture. Here are a few numbers followed by their Hebrew counterpart and the correlating meaning as found in the Bible:

1. **One** - *Aleph*: strength; ox; leader; first; first day of creation
2. **Two** - *Beht*: house or tent; sons and daughters; double portion; confirmation; witness
3. **Three** - *Gimel*: ripen; reward; trinity - Father God, Holy Spirit, Jesus Christ; a chord of three is strength
4. **Four** - *Dalet*: door; portal to Heaven; four winds; four corners of the earth; four seasons make a complete year
5. **Five** - *Hey*: grace; Torah; femininity; women have just as much inheritance in the instruction and teaching of the Word and spreading its message as men, which is pictured for us in Zelophehad's daughters (see Numbers 27:7)
6. **Six** - *Vav*: hook; nail; connect; beast; six usually refers to the works of man, but ideally represents sacrificial love and intimate knowledge with the Creator, when the latter is forsaken, only idolatry and flesh remain; sixth church of Revelation: Philadelphia (meaning *brotherly love*)

7. **Seven-** *Zayin*: wholeness; weapon; sword; completeness or perfection; shabbat, or the Sabbath day of rest is on the seventh day; Seven Spirits of God (see Revelation 5:6 and Isaiah 11:2). seven churches (see Revelation 1:4); wisdom has seven pillars (see Proverbs 9:1). seventh church of Revelation: Laodicea (meaning *justice* or *vengeance of the people*); the harlot in the book of Revelation rides a scarlet beast that has SEVEN heads, she is the epitome of one ruled by the image of the beast created on day six and the lusts of the flesh; instead of holding the holy shabbat kiddush cup (*holiness*), she has a cup full of abominations (see Proverbs 6:16-19)

8. **Eight** - *Chet*: new beginnings; a new order of creation and man's true "born again" event when he is resurrected from the dead into eternal life; circumcision of the heart through Christ and the receiving of the Holy Spirit (see Romans 2:28-29, Colossians 2:11-13); after the seven days of the Feast of Tabernacles there is an eighth day, called the "Last Great Day"

9. **Nine** - *Tet*: finality; judgment; harvest; nine fruits of the Spirit; the womb; ninth hour is the hour of prayer (Acts 3:1; 10:30); Yeshua will leave the 99 sheep to go after one (Matthew 18:12)

In the springtime, standing on my dock at our family cabin, also known as the Eagles Nest, I stood in awe as the sky took on jewel tone colors of pink and blue. The water appeared like glass that glistened in stillness to reflect the jewel tones of the sky. I had become so completely captivated by the arch of colors that moved from one side of the lake to the other that I nearly fell off the back of the dock. The rainbow became a ruby color that I had not seen before. The water reflected each color's radiance as the convergence of "on earth as it is in heaven" shined bright in a Genesis 9:11 moment that symbolized God's covenant love.

In Genesis, God tells Noah, "I will establish My covenant with you; and all flesh shall never again be cut off by the water of the flood, neither shall there again be a flood to destroy the earth" (Genesis 9:11). The covenant sign of a rainbow was spoken of several times in the scriptures that follow:

> And God said, "This is the sign of the covenant I am making between me and you and every living creature with you, a covenant for all generations to come: I have set my rainbow in the clouds, and it will be the sign of the covenant between me and the earth. Whenever I bring clouds over the earth and the rainbow appears in the clouds, I will remember my covenant between me and you and all living creatures of every kind. Never again will the waters become a flood to destroy all life. Whenever the rainbow appears in the clouds, I will see it and remember the everlasting covenant between God and all living creatures of every kind on the earth." (Genesis 9:12-16 NIV)

Colors of The Rainbow

The rainbow is also a sign of the throne room and the appearance of God. In Ezekiel the brightness of God is likened to a rainbow: "As the appearance of the rainbow in the clouds on a rainy day, so was the appearance of the surrounding radiance" (Ezekiel 1:28a). The apostle John uses the word rainbow to describe what he saw in the throne room: "And He who was sitting was like a jasper stone and a sardius in appearance; and there *was* a rainbow around the throne, like an emerald in appearance" (Revelation 4:3). John saw the rainbow before the judgement.

When the sign of God is manifested on earth, it shall be accompanied by a rainbow. The Spirit of God descended visibly out of the heavens before the prophet Ezekiel:

> Now above the expanse that was over their heads there was something resembling a throne, like lapis lazuli in appearance;

and on that which resembled a throne, high up, was a figure with the appearance of a man. Then I noticed from the appearance of His loins and upward something like glowing metal that looked like fire all around within it, and from the appearance of His loins and downward I saw something like fire; and there was a radiance around Him. As the appearance of the rainbow in the clouds on a rainy day, so was the appearance of the surrounding radiance. Such was the appearance of the likeness of the glory of the Lord. And when I saw it, I fell on my face and heard a voice speaking. (Ezekiel 1:26-28)

The likeness of the glory of the Lord is described in reference to the rainbow: the light, the colors, and the glory. Each of the seven colors of the rainbow also have meaning and new discoveries are being made to those meanings. In all actuality, prophecies are being played out right before our eyes.

Some scholars have likened the colors of the rainbow to the different millenniums. Now, if this is the case, it's possible we have begun moving into a new time, marked by a significant event. On December 6th, 2017, the United States formally recognized Jerusalem as the capital of Israel. Not coincidentally, the longest rainbow ever on record shined bright just one week before Jerusalem was recognized in what could be considered a new era, or most assuredly, what we can consider a sign from God. Recorded by two scientists in Taiwan, the rainbow shined for 8 hours and 58 minutes, not nine hours as some claimed.

One can choose to recognize the connection between the two events, or not, but the two incidents are absolutely connected and the timing of the rainbow is a divine instance.

Physicists at the Randall Monroe University in West Virginia have actually discovered an eighth color, said to be a basic color to the rainbow. The color, they say, is best thought of in similar terms to "grue" and "bleen," words used by linguists to better bring understanding to other languages seeking to differentiate between the colors of blue and green.

The awakening that we are in is accompanied by new colors that release new sounds, and new sounds that release the new colors. Science, created by God, is just catching up as He allows.

By separating white light by a glass prism, Isaac Newton is credited for naming the seven colors in the rainbow. He believed the seven colors were tied to the seven notes on the scale and the seven days of the week. Taking this all into account, if there is a new color God is allowing scientists to discover, what could that mean about sound, or even the days? The essence of awakening is coming into awareness of the reality of the Kingdom of God.

The 8th Day

The day the Israelites received the Promised Land was known as the "8th day." The day they crossed over the Jordan River was a new day. Further understanding concerning this day is provided in the book *The Jewish Way: Living the Holidays*, by Rabbi Irving Greenberg. Rabbi Irving tells us *(emphasis mine)*:

> When the seven days of Sukkot end, the Bible decrees yet another holiday, the Eighth Day of Assembly. The Rabbis interpreted this as an encore. After the High Holy Days, after the intense seven days of Sukkot and pilgrimage, the Jewish people (or, we should say, more accurately, "God's people") are about to leave, to scatter and return to their homes. God grows nostalgic, as it were, and pensive. The people of Israel will not come together again in such numbers until Passover six months hence. ***God will soon miss the sounds of music and pleasure and the unity of the people.***[5]

First of all, *Sukkot*, also known as the "Feast of Booths" or "Feast of Tabernacles," is one of the three biblically-based pilgrimage holidays. Thanksgiving is given for the fruit harvest and small hut-like structures are built. The huts (called *sukkah* meaning "one tent" or plural *sukkot*) were what the Jewish people lived in during the 40 years of travel through the wilderness exodus from Egypt. The sukkah, a temporary dwelling, also represents the fact that all existence is fragile, and therefore the Sukkot feast is a time to appreciate the shelter of our homes and our bodies.

God longs for the eighth day, a time when there is unity with His bride as it was in the garden. In that secret place, the tabernacle, there are songs of unity. The process of moving into the eighth day, the awakening into the fullness of the promises, can be painful at times, but worth it.

Native American Honor

In the spring of 2017, I was invited to attend what was called the Dakota Honoring. After the incredible weekend I had a better understanding of what honor and reconciliation can unlock. Not only was I there to better understand honor, but to also learn how the Native American people view the creation, the land and animals. It became clear that I was there to hear the sound of the drumbeat. The drumbeat sound once again reminded me of Grace and of all the other babies in Heaven who are making sound as they worship King Jesus. The sound of the drumbeat I heard that day was the same sound I had heard the night I read the Mississippi Letter.

There are many things I treasure about the Native American culture, including their reverence for nature that God creates, and the honor shown one to another. After listening to a man share a vision and a song he wrote, I learned that the sound of the drum beat is like the Creator's heartbeat, which represents and brings life.

The importance of land, the animals, and water was highlighted over and over again. As I listened to the stories, I was also awakened to the scriptures that Holy Spirit reminded me of:

Hear, O earth: behold, I am bringing disaster on this people, the fruit of their plans, because they have not listened to My words, and as for My law, they have rejected it also. (Jeremiah 6:19)

O land, land, land, hear the word of the Lord! (Jeremiah 22:29)

But now ask the beasts, and let them teach you; And the birds of the heavens, and let them tell you. Or speak to the earth, and let it teach you; And let the fish of the sea declare to you. Who among all these does not know that the hand of the Lord has done this, in whose hand is the life of every living thing, and the breath of all mankind? (Job 12:7-10)

Once again, in the summer month of June, not long after the Dakota Honoring, I saw another rainbow of color after visiting with the friend I had met at the honoring. She had included me in a post on social media that had to do rainbows, having an understanding of how God had been speaking to me. In that moment, another rainbow appeared. It was visible from the back of the cabin, but this time, there was another color I'd never seen before. I wondered if maybe this was the eighth color that danced in light before my eyes.

Eight means "new beginning." If we desire new beginnings, we must learn to honor God, ourselves, and each other. The things we think, the words we speak, and the actions that we take matter.

Months after the Dakota Honoring I had a dream of awakening. The dream came on September 18, just before the beginning of the Hebrew year 5778. In the dream, the morning of September 19, I was singing, but I was singing to the land. Prior to my singing, the land was disturbed and the solution was song. In a hunched over position, I sang down towards the ground so as to bring comfort. When I woke up, I couldn't stop thinking about the land wanting to be calmed and comforted.

That day, September 19, there was a 7.1 earthquake in Mexico.

After the discovery of the earthquake, I knew the Lord was again highlighting the significance of song and that it wasn't just people who would be comforted by song, but also the land.

One of the reasons for major earthquakes and volcanoes erupting is because the *land* itself is crying out. The land recognizes the time and the injustice that it wants to vomit out. The signs of earthquakes are the beginning of birth pains (see Matthew 24:7-8). The land recognizes the sons and daughters of God: "For the anxious longing of the creation waits eagerly for the revealing of the sons of God" (Romans 8:19), and the sons and daughters of God are awakening to the sounds they hear from around the throne.

With honor, we can see with understanding that there is value in each life, the animals, and the creation. Even trees swaying side-to-side know how to bring praise and honor to King Jesus, the Messiah.

Amborella Flower

The amborella flower has weathered the conditions of centuries. She is a flower that will certainly receive her crown. When the flower grows towards the sun, life blossoms. When you look towards the sun, you feel its warmth on your face. Warmth is an indicator for closeness and intimacy that is good. We must come near the *Son* to blossom.

The following is a statement that was created by the executive director of the Amborella House, a place that will cause restoration for many amborella, because the vision has been rooted in prayer:

> "The Amborella flower is the oldest living species in the world. It stands with simple beauty, growing and surviving in all conditions, displaying God's enduring love and His creation."

Many of us are like the amborella flower. We've gone through so much, dishonoring our bodies, our babies, and our brothers, but we've since grown and become restored. Even though we've been dishonored, we forgive because He showed us how. We've come to find the storyline has been sewn with grace and mercy.

Butterfly Confirmation

A symbol in my life that has represented freedom and confirmation to move forward is the butterfly. Prior to going to South Africa, and after much prayer, it was highlighted that I was to sell my prized Jeep Rubicon. That green vehicle had been with me in Montana and Minnesota, but this was a new season.

After listing the vehicle for sale, a buyer contacted me right away. In the midst of our exchange of papers and funds, I began to experience a moment of panic. I questioned if this was really the right thing to do. Maybe you know how this goes? You are absolutely led by God to do something, but then the "what if's" kick in.

As I pondered getting rid of this prized possession, a butterfly flew directly in front of me. Not only did the butterfly fly in front of me, but it hovered over me for what seemed like several minutes. In that confirming moment, I was reminded of freedom. Even more amazing is a friend had given me a bracelet with butterflies on it and told me to "follow the butterflies" a week prior to that moment.

The deal was done. The Jeep was sold.

A month later I was accepted into the 13th Floor Arts Ministry in South Africa. In a place that fanned the flame of creativity, biblical truth, identity and fellowship with brothers and sisters, awakening was my reality. The moments of refining and aligning with destiny were better than driving around in a silly old Jeep that represented the past anyway.

The Loon Call

Not only is the loon the state bird of Minnesota, but it is a majestic bird that teaches us a significant lesson about sound.

The loon, also called the great northern diver, is a bird who produces a beautiful sound to communicate. If you've ever heard a loon call, you know just how amazing the sound really is. Loons play hide and seek, as in, they know how to go undercover and move at the right time. Not everything they do is always out in the open for all to see. One loon may be on the top of the water making a sound to call for his loved one, and the other may be under the water only hearing a faint sound.

As they get closer to one another, the sounds get louder.

The common loon has four calls which can be placed into categories: hoots, wails, tremolos, and yodels. Some are soft and carry for only a short distance. Other calls travel over lakes for tremendous distance. When loon mates wail at each other they usually begin with a one-note call, then a two-note call, and may continue to a three-note wail if their mate does not respond. Eventually and hopefully, the loons will begin to alternate their signals. When there are sleeping loons who drift apart, it takes a vocal search for one another to awaken.

In addition to being a mysterious bird who makes a beautiful sound, loons also carry their babies on their backs for safety and comfort.

A generation of women, of mothers, are rising up to carry their young in safety and song.

Psalm 91:1 Reality

In the Native American culture, the appearance of white feathers signifies rebirth and new beginnings. Feathers are commonly worn on Native American headdresses to symbolize hope and faith. Eagle feathers were given to soldiers who returned from war, or, if there was great accomplishment to be recognized.

In the scriptures, feathers metaphorically represent loving care and protection. Feathers can also represent a fresh start in a spiritual sense, or that angels are near.

In Revelation 12:14 a woman is mentioned who receives the wings of a large eagle, which allows her to escape Satan and survive in a wilderness hideout for three and a half years. Here the eagle's wings represent swift getaway from danger that God provides for His people. One can speculate that John was watching the woman airlifted out of harm's way during a very dangerous time. The woman, who may likely represent the believers on earth as well as believing Israel, does, in fact, receive God's protection.

Protection in God's care is often best described in Psalm 91:

He who dwells in the shelter of the Most High will abide in the shadow of the Almighty. I will say to the Lord, "My refuge and my fortress, my God, in whom I trust!" For it is He who delivers you from the snare of the trapper and from the deadly pestilence. He will cover you with His pinions, and under His wings you may seek refuge; His faithfulness is a shield and bulwark. (Psalm 91:1-4)

Psalm 91 gives us the perfect picture of covering.

Bible heroes like David and Paul knew God does not necessarily provide an "umbrella bubble of protection" from trouble, but He may. Their lives were full of suffering and trials, but at the same time, they also had clear guidance and help from God. God was with them in everything.

As often as I've declared Psalm 91 over my life, there have still been troubles I've gotten myself into by not entering into the *secret place*. It's likely there were even times when I wasn't supposed to be delivered from trouble because the trouble was meant to refine and define me as a daughter of God.

Daniel's three friends told Nebuchadnezzar "God is able to deliver us but even if he doesn't, we will not serve your gods" (see Daniel 3:17-18). They knew that while God is *able* to deliver and that He *may* in specific cases, in some cases He does not keep us from trouble. It's not best for us and our development or restoration to be "saved" from a certain circumstances. If it was good enough for Jesus to learn obedience by the things He suffered (see Hebrews 5:8), then isn't it likely we too, will learn from trials?

The word used for *secret place* in Psalms 91:1 is the Hebrew word "satar." A secret place, or satar, shelters us and guides us. It is in satar that we learn the heart of God.

The Hebrew letters of satar are *samek, tav* and *resh.* If you look at the samek, it is like a rounded vessel with a cover, or shelter. Tav or taw represents the truth or knowledge of God. When we enter the taw, we enter into and act upon a knowledge of God that guides and provides restoration. The taw also represents guidance so we can make the best decision. We can enter this secret place by resh. Resh represents the Holy Spirit. It is the Holy Spirit who leads us into all truth and knowledge of God.

It is by dwelling in the *secret place* that we experience the sheltered place under the shadow of the Almighty.

"Each truth of God is a jewel which perfectly reflects all the other jewels in that net of God's knowledge. When we enter that secret place of God we begin to see each jewel of truth and it's reflections to all the other truths of God. Each truth of God is a shadow of all His other truths and to dwell in the shadow of God is to experience all the jewels of the knowledge of God. We may not comprehend all the knowledge of God but we will experience its shadow." [6]

— CHAIM BENTORAH

The signs and the symbols have been signposts along the way to bring assurance that we are on the right path. Just like the wise men followed a star in the sky, we are following the signs in awakening along the way to meet the Messiah face-to-face.

As our Father sings over us, we are hearing the sounds of Heaven get louder and louder. Music will always be a universal language, and when we sing in tune with the sounds Heaven is making, we will be drawn further into the presence of the Messiah. Sometimes we need to sing our way right back into the garden. For, in the garden, we recognize God in much of His creation.

Like the loons call back and forth out of longing, we too, will join with the choirs in Heaven, including the eternals, for the ultimate love song.

We will soon come to find that many of the signs and symbols

were pointing us in the direction of the Messiah, the one who satis-
fies our deepest longing.

> The Lord your God is with you, the Mighty Warrior who saves. He
> will take great delight in you; in his love he will no longer rebuke
> you, but will rejoice over you with singing. (Zephaniah 3:17 NIV)

SIGNS AND SYMBOLS KEY

1. What message did you learn from chapter six?

2. What are the signs and symbols that have been highlighted to you? What do these signs and symbols mean?

3. Write out three different scriptures on signs.

4. What did you learn about singing? What scriptures can you find in the Bible to support what you've learned?

5. What did you learn about Psalm 91:1? Where else in scripture is the Hebrew word "satar" used?

7

SONS AND DAUGHTERS OF DESTINY

HONOR KEY

At first people refuse to believe that a strange new thing can be done, then they begin to hope it can be done, then they see it can be done - then it is done and all the world wonders why it was not done centuries ago.

Frances Hodgson Burnett, *The Secret Garden*

When I was young, I had a recurring dream that I was running in a race. I could see the finish line, but I never finished. Not only did I not finish, but I fell within reach of crossing the finish line. From then on, once I began to really pay attention to my dreams, I felt a kind of fear that stemmed from not finishing the race.

The fear was debilitating. The feeling like I wasn't going to finish was even worse.

The good news is that the Lord does not give a spirit of fear, but of power, love, and a sound mind (see 2 Timothy 1:7). With that truth in mind, I prayed regarding that dream with the Word of God and eventually, learned how to enter into a place of rest.

According to the *American Heritage Dictionary,* the word "destiny" is defined as:

> 1. The inevitable or necessary fate to which a particular person or thing is destined; one's lot.
> 2. A predetermined course of events considered as something beyond human power of control: *"Marriage and hanging go by destiny" (Robert Burton).*
> 3. The power or agency thought to predetermine events: *Destiny brought them together.* [7]

Before we were even born, there were words written about our days. That's the thing about destiny, it's a predetermined course that we work out (see Philippians 2:12). After Jacob wrestled with God regarding his destiny, the Lord touched his hip. For the rest of his life he walked with a limp, which prophetically demonstrated dependence on God.

To wrestle with destiny is natural, but unless there is humility to go to God, the designer of dreams, we'll struggle with purpose, not knowing the direction to take. We won't be distracted by comparison or a lack of understanding of purpose if we have an interdependence *on* God.

Independence *from* God can be likened to pride. The stubborn man or woman ignores God, His good guidance and His loving correction. As we look to our Maker, He is the One who will draw each one of us towards destiny. We can rest in the truth that His faithfulness will pull us through. It is not destiny to fall within reach of the finish line, nor is it destiny to live in fear.

> Whatever God has promised gets stamped with the Yes of Jesus. In him, this is what we preach and pray, the great Amen, God's Yes and our Yes together, gloriously evident. God affirms us, making us a sure thing in Christ, putting his Yes within us. By his Spirit he

has stamped us with his eternal pledge - a sure beginning of what he is *destined* to complete. (2 Corinthians 1:20-22 MSG *emphasis mine*)

Angels Assist Your Destiny

After a special fall conference, a prayer hike to the high point of Minnesota was in order. As we walked out the prayer hike, our summit to the peak was enriched through song, declarations of truth over Minnesota and a long hike back to the car in the dark of the north woods.

Divine angelic assistance helped light up the path. There were large footprints in the snow which completely messed with my thinking. Of course, in the natural mind, I kept thinking someone had hiked the trail before us. It was strange that the footprints prints were not there on our summit up Eagle Mountain. We hiked too late in the day for anyone else to be on the trail. On our way back, the large footprints blazed the trail for us in light. Getting back was a miracle that came with assistance.

Much of our hike was centered in worship.

Angels assemble around anointed worship.

While in Israel, during one of the most incredible times of worship, a time of sound coming only from the voices of the people who gathered together, I began to sense the presence of an angel. As I drew what I was seeing and wrote out the words in Revelation 22, others made remarks of an angel being present in the room. Pictures flashed in my mind of water flowing through the streets in Jerusalem.

Each one of us has been assigned with angels. The author of Hebrews wrote: "Are they not all ministering spirits, sent out to render service for the sake of those who will inherit salvation?" (Hebrews 1:14) The assistance of angels will help us move along the course of destiny and into our inheritance. To see destiny come to fullness, assistance is necessary. We were not meant to do life alone.

In my time of independence, especially when struggling with drug use, there were several times when the demonic would rage. Demonic forces are fallen angels. These evil spirits will be taken down with Lucifer, who attempted to elevate himself. Just as those fallen angels go on assignment, there are angels on assignment from Christ, who is "the head over every power and authority" (see Colossians 1:18, 2:10). There are far more angels that are assisting us for the good. The demonic angels (demons), deemed as pestilence, are destined for the pit.

Angels are never to be worshiped. In Revelation 19:10 the apostle John is told by an angel *not* to fall at his feet. But, angels do assist heirs of salvation, you and I, to carry out God's commands:

> In Judges 6, the "angel" of the Lord appeared to Gideon. For seven straight years the Midianites raided the people of God and stole their harvests. They were greatly impoverished because of it, but it was time to stop the raiding and the lost harvests. It was time to shift into gathering harvests, and clearly an angel assisted that assignment. The angel was instrumental in shifting Gideon from a passive, intimidated, and desolate existence into a mighty leader of great valor who, with supernatural help, took 300 men and killed 15,000 Midianite warriors. Gideon, a remnant, and angels brought by the harvest. (Dr. Tim Sheets, *Angel Armies*) [8]

I've needed help to stop the lack, the loss and the passivity. Any mighty move of justice is not going to happen without the assistance of the angel armies. Angels are meant to assist us towards destiny.

Esther the Prophet

In 2009 a prophet named Esther from Africa was sent to our family through divine alignment for the purpose of destiny.

While Esther stayed with us, she recognized the battle that my dad was facing. After some time at our home and conversations with my dad, she asked if she could pray. With my dad's permission, we all gathered near him to pray with nothing but love. Her words of prayer came straight from the Father.

After Esther prayed, my dad looked up from where he was sitting with a smile on his face and a few genuine tears in his eyes. We all knew Esther was sent from the Lord to minister God's unconditional love to all of us, including my dad. Her presence in our home taught me to love and honor him, especially in the midst of alcoholism. Alcoholism was the entanglement that was trying to take his life and destroy our family.

When Esther looked at him and spoke to him, even if he'd been drinking, there was honor in both her verbal and her non-verbal communication. Once, at the dinner table, she looked at him and said, "Since you are the head of this household, why don't you lead us in prayer?" My dad paused for a moment, as we all did, and then he proceeded to pray. The prayer was real, genuine and straight from the heart. It wasn't one of those religious prayers of repeated words with a cold heart. Everyone could feel the presence of God in the room. Honor was the key that ushered us into a restoration moment.

Esther is now in prison for rightly speaking up while preaching a message at a church in Kigali, Africa. In 2016, Esther went with police to answer questions about her sermon. She has been incarcerated since that time. Esther once told her story of surviving the Rwandan genocide and her journey to forgiveness, not only here in the States, but in her country of Africa. Through her testimony, hardened criminals have opened their hearts to the gospel.

She is now bringing hope to 1,200 new prisoners, herself as one of them, in Ngoma prison.

For this reason I endure all things for the sake of those who are chosen, so that they also may obtain the salvation which is in Christ Jesus and with it eternal glory. (2 Timothy 2:10)

The Family Destiny

Sometimes we get the opportunity to join the forces of heaven in an all-out war on what comes to destroy the family. We do not need to fully accept a family member's "alcoholism," passed on from the previous generations in a spiritual way. The thought that nothing can be done is not biblical. I refuse to sit back and do nothing. Of course, there comes a time when boundaries are necessary for personal restoration, but that doesn't stop a move of the Holy Spirit and the angels that assemble around worship.

One of my favorite things to do is to compose songs at the piano for the purpose of worship. Many of the songs are Spirit-led, birthed out of a time with God. When I first came out of treatment for drugs and alcohol, back into the home of my family, I spent a lot of time at the piano. Those times of worship created a spiritual atmosphere that not only invited angels but also sent the darkness fleeing.

During the same season when Esther came into our lives, my husband and I stayed at my family's home. Praying together one afternoon, I was led to understand how alcoholism had been generational. Understanding and love for my dear dad flowed in my heart as God's presence invaded our space. The Lord led me to forgive him. Even though he never intentionally brought harm, the Lord revealed there was anger in my heart. Alcohol stole his attention in my youth, so more than anything I longed for a relationship.

I hated what alcohol was doing.

Alcohol destroys not only the person, but the person's family as well. There is a spirit of intoxication connected to alcoholism which can carry over through different generations unless dealt with in the only way that will actually end the struggle once and for all - belief, the blood of Jesus Christ, and baptism of the Holy Spirit:

Who is the one who overcomes the world, but he who believes that Jesus is the Son of God? This is the One who came by water and blood, Jesus Christ; not with the water only, but with the water and with the blood. It is the Spirit who testifies, because the

Spirit is the truth. For there are three that testify: the Spirit and the water and the blood; and the three are in agreement. (1 John 5:5-8)

The one who believes is the overcomer.

Through a series of bizarre spiritual happenings, my dad got sober. He'd had enough. He hit his rock bottom moment and then he believed.

In time, and when led by the Holy Spirit, I asked my dad to forgive me. Actions backed up those words before I was led to ask. Growing up, I had acted out in rebellion and was disrespectful. Thank goodness destiny has a way of turning us around. In the book of Isaiah we are told that God loves us and that we are precious and honored in His sight. Only with the lens of love that God gives can we truly show the kind of honor that unlocks destiny.

Over the years, my husband and my dad have grown close. Through their relationship, they have both received healing. My husband and my dad both lost their dads when they were young. They've shared some of the same hurts and struggles, but have also shared in some of the same overcoming victories, like getting sober, building and owning businesses, growing in faith, and being men of honor who have chosen to get better.

All men and women are broken outside of the life of Christ. As the saying goes, "hurt people, hurt people." Each one of us can wrestle with feelings of being hurt, and yet, we can also find healing in one good Father.

A Dance of Destiny

Science tells us that the relationship between a father and child deeply impacts a child's long-term development in many critical ways. A father's influence in his daughter's life shapes her self-esteem, self-image, confidence, and opinions of men. Children with involved fathers are less likely to experience depression and teen pregnancy, or to engage in risky behaviors such as substance use.

When vulnerability factors decrease, the risk of being exploited or addicted becomes less. Clearly, a key to decreasing the statistics of exploitation and problematic substance use is to strengthen the family, including the father-daughter relationship.

During a destiny-type weekend to build the father-daughter relationship, little girls danced with their dads at our organization's first Daddy Daughter Dance on May 13, 2017. Before the dance began, my dad and I took our first photo together, just the two of us, since 1984. I felt proud to stand next to him. We both smiled from ear to ear.

At the dance, little girls created gifts and answered questions so their dads would know their love language (i.e. words of affirmation, quality time, etc). A brother in Christ, Mike, a co-founder of Action169, spoke a message about how the eagle can be likened to the man who is focused and ready to better raise up his young.

This was also a day that I had the privilege of sharing a letter from the heart of a daughter which highlighted the significance of a father in a daughter's life. When I looked out to those I was speaking to, I saw men of honor who were raising up their daughters, working hard to provide, protect and communicate love in the best way they each knew how. This was a group of Gideons, sons of God, with focused vision to raise up their daughters dependent on the one good Father.

The fathers who were present were seeking to fight for their daughters more than the culture.

On May 12, 2018, there was yet another dance, a Daughters of Destiny Dance. Each father spoke a truthful word affirmation to call out the destiny in his little girl as he placed a crown-like a garland of grace upon her head. Each little girl looked up at her dad to see a father who would do his very best to raise her up.

The 3rd Daddy Daughter Dance on May 4, 2019, was centered upon the truth that we are seated in Christ, each one of us who has believed and received the Lord as our personal Savior. In the garden, there is a seated position of royalty that comes with recognizing identity. Sometimes we need to be reminded of who we are in Christ. Gideon, for example, needed to be reminded of who he was, but not before he was reminded of Who was with him.

A New Move of Gideon

In the story of Gideon, "The angel of the Lord appeared to him and said to him, 'The Lord is with you, O valiant warrior'" (Judges 6:12). This message came at a time when Gideon was hiding in a wine press. How many of us have hidden in the wine press only to be called out towards something better? Destiny purpose is always better than hiding, but we often need to be reminded of Whose we are and what we are capable of.

The people who were brought out of slavery had began to worship idols and false gods when that angel appeared to Gideon. They looked away from the one true God and ignored His good direction in their lives. In the depths of oppression they called out and God sent them a prophet, the man Gideon. Even though Gideon hid, God called out the true nature of His son with just a few words. And this is what we, His sons and daughters, do when we call forth the true nature of others.

In an awakening, honor and action, paired with words that are spoken, unlock destiny. The sons of God are aligning with who they really are in a new justice move that is awakening many to the Father's heart like in Malachi 4:6. The verse tells us that hearts are turning towards one another in reverence.

A new move of *Gideon* is emerging.

Honor unlocks destiny.

A Women's Move of Deborahs

Sons like *Barak* are going to war to change culture.

Daughters like *Deborah* are showing honor and speaking out words of encouragement.

Remember, Deborah was a prophetess to Israel. In Judges we can read about her responsibilities ranging from settling disputes, being a wife and leading in a war. She knew her purpose and didn't waste time.

Deborah means "to speak or promise," but there is more to know about who she was:

> "Deborah's very name is the key to understanding her. The essence of her name, 'honeybee,' is the essence of the anointing that will rest on women. Just as bees swarm behind a leader, women will have new leadership responsibilities in the church and will be recognized as prophets who teach and guide the body of Christ. The sting of a bee is bitterly painful, yet its honey is sweet, so will women who have godly dispositions, demonstrate sweet words of wisdom to those they influence and a deadly stinger the enemies of God." (*The Deborah Anointing*, Michelle McClain-Walters) [9]

Daughters of God like Deborah are rising up in this hour and they do not slander the sons of God around them. They build them up and speak to the true nature because they recognize identity.

Barak, the military commander in the book of Judges, would not go to war unless Deborah came with him. Deborah spoke encouragement when she said to Barak, "Arise! For this is the day in which the Lord has given Sisera into your hands; behold, the Lord has gone out before you" (see Judges 4:14). Sisters, sometimes we need to remind our brothers in Christ *Who* goes before them. Amazingly, we can do this in our words, our actions and prayers. We can do this by showing honor. There is far too much slander going on in the worldly culture. We are called to oppose aligning ourselves with the accuser of the brethren.

It took the prophetic leadership of Deborah and the military leadership of Barak to win the war. Barak realized Deborah's potential to lead in the midst of crises. Her prophetic gift to inspire and activate, coupled with Barak's military skills made for a great team.

Together, they defeated the Canaanite armies.

Together they sang of victory, which almost seems like a prophetic song. Maybe they sang the song before or during the war to awaken themselves:

Awake, awake, Deborah; Awake, awake, sing a song! Arise, Barak, and take away your captives, O son of Abinoam. (Judges 5:12)

Song Unifies and Wins

In 2015 the Lord gave me a dream that gave hope. He wanted to change my thoughts about not finishing the race. The dream came after a time of praying about the riots happening at that time, many of which were race-related and rooted in fear and hatred. It didn't make sense. I thought we'd already moved past racism.

The dream showed a scene of a race where many people were getting ready to run. I was near the back of the line, which is where I usually start my 5k's. Suddenly, a shofar sounded loudly. The sound somehow pulled me towards the front of the line. I didn't just move to the frontline, I flew past it. Others began to run. Instead of running a normal race, I was running in and out of people's homes along the route. In the final scene of the dream, I was in the home of an African American family. Together, we were singing. The song brought unity. Holding their baby, I looked into his big brown eyes I sang, "Yes, Jesus loves you."

The song was rewritten the next day, with a bit of southern kick that would continue to come up over the next several years.

Not long after the dream, I ended up on the *Field of Dreams* former movie set in Iowa after an event. It was a God-ordained destiny moment where I joined papa Lou Engle to walk the bases, pray and sing with the group "David's Tent" who is living out a mission of 24 hour worship in Washington DC.

The Field of Dreams day was a Malachi 4:6 moment. It was

God's dream for a spiritual father to the nation, a daughter, and a David's tent to sing, pray and make declarations over the nation. There were others there that day, and each one was in a prophetic destiny moment. In unison we sang *Yes, Jesus Loves Me* like drawing the bride of Christ back to her first love, Jesus.

In his book *Nazirite DNA*, Lou wrote about Elijah. He wrote of a novel he once read and what was highlighted to him on p.169. Papa Lou shares that God was shouting at him:

> "I am raising up Nazirites who will set their face to tear down the altars of pornography and sexual immorality in the land. They have made the vow to stand against abortion and take care of the pregnant mother. They burn for adoption and they challenge sex trafficking." [10]

The shouting Lou referred to is getting louder and louder. Can you hear the alarms?

The song *Yes, Jesus Loves Me* was not only sung there in Iowa with a dream team, but on college campus and churches as a part of the Action169 Call to Action events. My favorite of all places to sing any songs or hear the voices of others singing is on outreach in the strip clubs. Songs bring unity and around worship, angels gather.

If you build it, He will come.

The Moses Song

Before Joshua led the people into the Promised Land, and right before Moses passed on the mantle of leadership, God taught Moses an awakening song in a day. God told Moses:

> "Now therefore, write this song for yourselves, and teach it to the sons of Israel; put it on their lips, so that this song may be a witness for Me against the sons of Israel. For when I bring them into the land flowing with milk and honey, which I swore to

their fathers, and they have eaten and are satisfied and become prosperous, then they will turn to other gods and serve them, and spurn Me and break My covenant. Then it shall come about, when many evils and troubles have come upon them, that this song will testify before them as a witness (for it shall not be forgotten from the lips of their descendants); for I know their intent which they are developing today, before I have brought them into the land which I swore." (Deuteronomy 31:19-21)

With God's help in a two-fold promise, Moses taught the people of Israel a song in a short period of time. Moses instructed a song that brought to mind the words of God's instructions that would guide them on the right path of righteousness.

Awake! Awake!

Like God taught Moses a song to awaken the people, so now is Holy Spirit teaching a song of awakening to His sons and daughters. Song will unify the bride of Christ and awaken her to show honor. Being disciples of Jesus, we step into destiny, and honor is one of the keys that unlocks the door.

Learning to become a disciple of Jesus has meant saying farewell to everything we might normally depend on, or find our identity in: family, friends, money, career, worldly honor, or prestige. Depending on God has meant seeking counsel from Him, His Living Word, and the Holy Spirit. We do not rely on the world that calls evil good and good evil. Sometimes it may take a crisis, or even a seeming disaster to bring us to the place where we fully acknowledge dependence on God. When this happens, we move into destiny.

Proverbs speaks of a *crown of beauty* likened to wisdom, and that the beginning of wisdom is the reverence of God and the good instruction He gives: "She (wisdom) will place on your head a garland of grace; She will present you with a crown of beauty" (Proverbs 4:9). We'll be carried through to the finish line by His strength and good instruction in what is marked as a predetermined course of destiny in which, "He who began a good work in you will perfect it until the day of Christ Jesus." (Philippians 1:6b)

> Brethren, I do not regard myself as having laid hold of it yet; but one thing I do: forgetting what lies behind and reaching forward to what lies ahead, I press on toward the goal for the prize of the upward call of God in Christ Jesus. (Philippians 3:13-14)

HONOR KEY

1. What scriptures can you find regarding destiny and honor? Write them in your journal and speak them out loud.

2. What scriptures can you find regarding wisdom? Write them in your journal and speak them out loud.

3. When was a time in which you were living independently of God?

4. How are you now living dependent or interdependent on God?

5. Why did God teach Moses a song according to Deuteronomy 31:19-21?

6. What is a practical way of showing someone honor? How can you honor God?

Father God,

You are a good, good Abba. Thank You for Truth. Thank You for Your Living Word, which guides my feet. Thank You for destiny and the plans You have for me. Father, teach me to love, honor and do Your will. Thank You for a Counselor, the Holy Spirit. Father, I desire to stay within the boundary lines that bring me into my inheritance, into the fullness of the garden. Give me eagle's vision, to remain focused on You. Lord, teach me how to show love and honor in all that I do.

In the name of Jesus, Amen

8

KEY OF DAVID

WORSHIP KEY

I know your deeds. Behold, I have put before you an open door which no one can shut, because you have a little power, and have kept My word, and have not denied My name.

Revelation 3:8

A key indicates access, authority and entrance. Keys can be likened to knowledge, which, if acted upon, can allow entrance into the fullness of the garden. However, unless the key is actually utilized, it won't do any good. Keys to unlocking the garden are given to those who believe, receive, and then take action.

At some point, disobedience will lead to a hardened heart. Jesus rebuked the Pharisees who hid knowledge from the people. He said, "Woe to you lawyers! For you have taken away the key of knowledge; you yourselves did not enter, and you hindered those who were entering" (Luke 11:52).

Notice how Jesus spoke of *knowledge* as a *key* and said that there was a way to *enter*?

Keys allow us entry into the Kingdom of God, making *on earth as it is in heaven* a realized reality.

After Peter's confession of Christ's identity, Jesus said, "I will give you the keys of the kingdom of heaven; and whatever you bind on earth shall have been bound in heaven, and whatever you loose on earth shall have been loosed in heaven" (Matthew 16:19). Peter was able to bind and loose because he had unlocked the truth of Jesus. What a treasure to know Jesus the Messiah, and to live out what He taught with the aid of the best Counselor, the Holy Spirit.

In relationship with Yeshua, the One who is the true steward of the Kingdom of Heaven, we have access to the greatest treasures of wisdom, which bring us into healing, wholeness, and restoration.

Before I married Corey, I had no idea the treasures of marriage that would soon be revealed if I chose love and stewarded my marriage well. Proper stewardship of what has been entrusted to us takes responsibility. We've been given truths like treasure and we are to steward them well.

King David

King David, known as a man after God's own heart, played music in the secret place, and he did so skillfully. In the secret place, he worshiped with sounds and songs that were pleasing to the Lord. The sounds he played were also healing for David's body, soul, and spirit.

King David was a man of success, yet, like each one of us, he also fell short in some areas of life. While he began in humble beginnings as a shepherd boy, he was eventually promoted to king. Regardless of his shortcomings, he was given specific skills and anointed as king in a lineage that would never end.

Before David was anointed as king, he was brought into the courts of King Saul to play the lyre, which is similar to a harp. In 1 Samuel 16:18, David is spoken of in the following order of characteristics, which were divinely recognized and spoken of by King Saul's servants:

1. Skillful in playing music
2. Man of valor
3. Man of war
4. Prudent in speech
5. Man of good presence
6. The Lord is with him

The list of good qualities was made possible because the Lord was with David, and David stewarded his talents well. Even when he messed up and took another man's wife (a decision which had devastating results), the Lord never left David.

At one time, King Saul had been pleased by David's musical giftings. David would play his lyre and the tormenting spirits that harassed Saul went away. Eventually, Saul decided he didn't like how recognized David was becoming due to his success. David learned what it was like to run for his life.

Throughout trial or victory, war or peace, David continued to go to the secret place during set aside times to worship God. David never reacted towards Saul with a heart of revenge. He did, however, raise up a mighty army.

With power from God, David defeated those in his path. He first would ask God for permission and instructions before going into battle (see 2 Samuel 5:22-23). God honored and rewarded the obedience of David and gave him *keys* to make a difference in his domain.

David's worship was an expression of his heart towards God which played out in different ways throughout his life. Worship with music and song was an aspect of this, but it was also about his hunger and thirst for God, and the way he lived his life in pursuit of God.

Hallelujah Sound and Song

Before Corey and I got married, God gave me a confirming dream. In the dream, I was sitting at a beautiful grand piano on the ground level floor in the middle of a circular room. Above me were different levels and each floor had a balcony. As far up as I could see, each balcony level had angels. The angels were singing, "Hallelujah" over and over again. I was singing with them, but my attention was not on them. What stood out was that Corey was sitting at the piano with me.

We faced the piano to play music together, along with the angels. We had joined in with the sound of the angels, which was like a choir of voices, beautiful and all for the One whom we were singing for - Jesus, Yeshua. He was sitting on the bench with us. I could hear the song in the dream, and the sounds were all for Him. What I love about the dream is that He was sitting with us, and not away from us.

Hallelujah is a Hebrew word meaning "praise ye YAH (Yahweh)." The word hallelujah in Revelation 19 is sung by a multitude that has gathered before the throne of God, in His immediate presence. In a victory celebration, all of Heaven renders praise as a song of thanksgiving is uttered by all who have united to worship the only One deserving.

God's righteous victory over His enemies (Revelation 19:1-2), His sovereignty (vs. 4–6), and His eternal communion with His people (v. 7) are all reasons to sing. The sound of the outpouring of praise and worship is so overwhelming that the apostle John can only describe it as "like a great multitude, like the roar of rushing waters and like loud peals of thunder" (see Revelation 19:6).

So great is the rejoicing by God's people at the wedding feast of the Bridegroom (Christ) and the bride (the church) that *hallelujah* is the only word magnificent enough to express it. Handel's version of the great chorus in Heaven, as glorious as the song is, is only a foreshadowing of the magnificence that will be expressed by the heavenly chorus as we sing, "Hallelujah, for the Lord God omnipotent reigns!"

The song Hallelujah by Handel was sung in Israel on May 21, 2017 over the week of celebrations honoring the 70th anniversary of Israel becoming a nation. This was a special time of celebration in Israel held in the sacred city of Jerusalem. Many came together to sing and celebrate, including the 45th president of the United States and his wife.

The beautiful song that was sung in Israel was not the only thing that sounded through the airwaves. While thousands worshiped Adonai and gave tribute to Israel in celebration near the City of David in Jerusalem, that day was also a day of grieving elsewhere in the world. The enemy made a way into a place the next day where 22 young women lost their lives.

May 22nd

On May 22, 2017, 22 people were tragically killed in Manchester, London at an Ariana Grande concert. This was a concert where mostly women, many either moms or daughters, gathered to see the musician perform.

The name *Ari* means "lioness" and in Hebrew, the name *Ariana* means "holy."

The attack itself indicates the rage of an enemy.

A mocking and destructive spirit acted out. The criminal seeks to mimic what is holy and beautiful - the ones created in God's image who can worship Adonai in the way they live their lives and by their praises in song and voice. Criminals bring confusion, dissonance and perversion. A criminal acts out when their time is short.

A criminal also seeks to distract.

Sound, Tones and a Key of David

Some of this chapter happened to be written on May 22, 2017. On that day, I finally cracked open a book that had been sitting on my shelf for months. After hearing me talk incessantly about sounds and tones, my dear friend told me it was time to read the book.

I had just returned from a weekend away at the northern-most border, where I spent the weekend with a group of women. Being a part of that gathering was strategic, as there was a key of knowledge that God would reveal before I read the book *Wholetones*.

Before May 22nd and the weekend away up north, I dreamt of being in a school on the third floor. In the dream, I broke through to the fourth floor while worshiping Jesus. Worship causes break-through. On that next level there were musical instruments. The instruments were new and had never been played before. The dream was recorded in my journal, and expectancy for the dream to make sense was tucked inside my heart.

Interestingly, the weekend of the gathering we stayed in an old school, exactly like in my dream. During the long drive there, I asked God what the purpose of my going would be. While I had previously prayed and had received peace about going, I took advantage of the drive that gave time for prayer. The Lord impressed upon me that He was going to "unlock a tone of Heaven." It goes without saying that in order to unlock something, one must have a key. There was nothing else to be done but pray and expect something divine to happen. Eventually, the divine began to unfold like a mystery waiting to be discovered.

Once I arrived, and after a time of worship, my attention was drawn to certain tones and frequencies of music notes. Prior to that weekend, the numbers 444 and 777 had been continually high-lighted. I soon discovered why. Searching through music notes and reading about frequencies, my attention was drawn to A4. The frequency of A4 is 444 and the wavelength was 777. Fascinated with this note, and learning about wavelength or vibration of sound, I found that I had been looking at a chart tuning A to a 444Hz instead of the standard 440Hz.

Music, and all sound, generates energy, which can be referred to, and thought of, as vibrations. It is a scientific fact that all matter, including humans, plants and even water gives off vibrations. A hertz or frequency is a pitch to which a note can be tuned towards. Simply put, a sound's pitch gives off energy or vibrations.

Before the standardization of 440hz, musicians tuned towards other frequencies. Think of it this way: when the early church played music or sang songs, they weren't tuning to 440hz. Over the centuries things have changed. The changes that brought standardization brought discord. Further study into why the pitch was changed and who changed it reveals why things should not have been changed. Instruments that are tuned to a 440 are actually tuned to the *wrong* frequency. This is a distraction from what could be better, more pure, and harmonious.

There was an actual key, or frequency, which King David tuned his instrument towards, and it was not 440hz. After my Spirit-led discovery of numbers, I was inspired to share the information with one of the members of the round table discussion, who also happens to be a musician.

While sitting at a piano, our conversation centered upon the colors and sounds of Heaven. As we worshiped God together, we also fumbled around the piano keys of different notes. We concluded that there needs to be a different note or a note somewhere in-between A and A sharp or B flat. My prayer mama Ruth, who had been standing nearby, pipped in and asked, "Have you read the book *Wholetones* yet?"

When I got home on May 22, I pulled the book from the shelf to read what the Lord had begun to highlight. He knew I would gradually comprehend these concepts, thanks to Holy Spirit and the revelations given to musician and author of *Wholetones*, Michael Tyrrell. This chapter would not be complete with reference to his work.

In *Wholetones*, Michael wrote about the key of David, which he identified as the A note tuned to a 444Hz, as was divinely revealed to him. The author wrote in depth and with keen understanding about sounds and frequencies, the impact, and the key that David likely played in on his lyre.

The call to action of what Michael wrote and what it means for the body of Christ is a key to entering into the fullness of the gardens of our lives. Holy Spirit is granting revelation to prepare the body of Christ to awaken, and song is a significant aspect of the awakening.

Picking up on what Holy Spirit was drawing my attention towards and learning from Michael's book, I wanted to tune to 444hz. This could not be done at my piano, but the Lord connected me with a Jewish man who could build a harp. Of course, I asked if he would tune the harp to 444hz, although this was something I could eventually learn to do myself. Through our conversations, he told me he was led to carve the Shin letter, which is the 21st letter of the Hebrew aleph-bet onto my harp.

The Shin letter carved on my harp was the four-pronged Shin, which led to an even deeper journey into what God is revealing. *Shin* means "fire and transformation," and can be likened to purifying and changing the condition of life. The four-lined Shin is the *Shin of the Luchos*, or the "tablets of the ten commandments." The four lines represent the awesomeness and holiness of the engraving of God's word into physical stone. Because the new covenant converges with the old covenant in Christ, His ways are now engraved upon our hearts:

> You are our letter, written in our hearts, known and read by all men; being manifested that you are a letter of Christ, cared for by us, written not with ink but with the Spirit of the living God, not on tablets of stone but on tablets of human hearts. (2 Corinthians 3:2-3)

> You shall love the Lord your God with all your heart and with all your soul and with all your might. These words, which I am commanding you today, shall be on your heart...You shall bind them as a sign on your hand... (Deuteronomy 6:5-6, 8a)

In Hebrew and Greek, the heart is the center of the mind, emotions, will, desires, etc. God writing His new covenant law in our hearts is a metaphor meaning He will regenerate our hearts to remember, love, and obey His laws. He writes His good Word on our hearts so that we act in accordance to what is pleasing to Him, and what brings life for us. Remember, Jesus is the fulfillment of the law, and He is the Word made flesh.

Jesus is the Word of God (see John 1:1).

Christ within leads us into the fullness of the garden of our lives. With Christ within, we are led to act in a way that is healthy, loving, kind, and good. We experience the kind of restoration that is spoken of in Isaiah:

> Is this not the fast which I choose, to loosen the bonds of wickedness, to undo the bands of the yoke, and to let the oppressed go free and break every yoke? Is it not to divide your bread with the hungry and bring the homeless poor into the house; When you see the naked, to cover him; And not to hide yourself from your own flesh? Then your light will break out like the dawn, and your recovery will speedily spring forth; And your righteousness will go before you; The glory of the Lord will be your rear guard. (Isaiah 58:6-8)

True worshipers worship in spirit and in truth. True worshipers show love, for they know how much they are loved. More important than the hertz in which we worship is the *spirit* in which we worship. How we sound does not affect God. What impacts His heart is the heart in which we worship. We do not want to become legalistic.

The person who walks in obedience through righteousness will respond differently than the person who walks in legalism when they fail. When dealing with shortcomings, a legalistic man will look internally and try to do better. On the contrary, when dealing with shortcomings and sin, a righteous man will look to Jesus, change direction, and carry on, knowing there is perfection in weakness and that His grace is sufficient (see 2 Corinthians 12:9).

My harp teacher's patience with me has been impeccable. Once we got past the reasons why we would be changing the pitch, it was smooth sailing. I still have much to learn, but I'm reminded of God's patience and love for His children who pursue the mysteries of His Kingdom.

Your Voice and Song is Key

Music is a universal language that gives off energy in vibrations, whether it be calming, chaotic, peaceful, or frenzied. We would benefit in changing the pitch, or what is referred to as the standard tone, in which instruments are tuned, even if the music industry standard says otherwise.

No matter what, *you*, with *your* voice and *your* song, can bring life-breathing worship to God as a pleasing fragrance. The words you speak truly influence and affect that which is around you, including yourself, so speak love. God is enthroned on our praises, and sound clearly has an effect on body, soul and spirit, so *of course* worship is a key of restoration. We must remember that worship is not just about song, but how we live our lives. We must steward well the revelations God shows us.

Just like I heard a drumbeat when I read about my daughter being in Heaven, my husband and I also heard the same drumbeat sound when we hiked Boundary Peak on September 12, 2017.

To have boundary lines means there is a path and way that leads to life. Outside the boundary lines, there is confusion and a lack of safety. Outside the boundary lines there are thistles and thorns.

> The boundary lines have fallen for me in pleasant places; surely I have a delightful inheritance. (Psalm 16:6 NIV)

The way into the fullness of restoration is within the boundary lines that lead into inheritance, the garden. We can take action by utilizing the keys we've been given, and not be like those who listen to the Word, but do not take action.

How blessed is the man who finds wisdom and the man who gains understanding. For her profit is better than the profit of silver and her gain better than fine gold. (Proverbs 3:13-14)

New Songs of Awakening

The books of songs in Heaven are opening and being received.

Songs are being sung, and the sons and daughters of God are beginning to hear these sounds. Holy sons and daughters of God are rising up and singing the song of the Lion of the Tribe of Judah and of the Lamb of God, tuned to the *key of David*, singing in spirit and truth.

The enemy has tried to silence the daughters of God by intimidation, seducing, sedating, and silencing us. And yet, we have victory as we tune our own voices to a harmony which vibrates through the frame, opening the body and soul to healing as we worship King Jesus. He, Himself, is harmony. Cornelius Van Dalen once said, "One can only come to harmony in life by attuning to that which is harmonious. Discord does not heal."

Each tribe of Israel is represented by a gemstone and a color. Deborah from the book of Judges is from the tribe of Issachar, a tribe represented by the blue sapphire.

I propose to you that there is an orchestrated army of angels that go before many anointed Deborahs in this hour. There is a release of a heaven-tone sound that is sapphire blue and likened to water, which brings awakening and washing. Daughters of God are rising up with good judgement and discernment in these times. They sing to awaken themselves from the deceit and lethargy of the culture that seduces, sedates, and silences.

Garden Zion Entrance

King David, the worshipping psalmist and war hero, was a man who held a key that gave him access to the secret place. His royal position, domain, and seat came with many responsibilities. In our day and age, he could have received a diagnosis of PTSD if it weren't for his practice of rest and devotion, as well as skillfully playing music in pursuit of God. Although he was a man who went to war, he knew the rest of God. He hungered and thirsted for God, and God gave him great favor, so much so that he was made king of Israel. David knew that having music and musicians around was important, and so, he appointed 24 groups of 12 musicians (a total of 880) who were set apart for prophetic worship.

We can find encouragement in David's story. For those of us who know we've been in a war, we can also rest. Life, in all of its responsibilities, is done best from a place of rest.

David knew the secret of devotion and getting into a place of solitude, alone with God. We must know how to quiet ourselves before God, for this is also the essence of worship. David knew the refreshing that came from silence, as well making sound to bring worship to God. As we learned in an earlier chapter, singing changes the brain of one who has experienced trauma or who is feeling fear. When David went into the secret place, he was able to come out and manage his domain with divine wisdom.

We are invited to come into the secret place, to meet with God, and be embraced by Him. We are then responsible with what's been entrusted to us, whether it be time, talent or treasure.

Deep calls out to deep, but to develop depth one must go into the depths of God's presence. David's pursuit of God demonstrated his knowing and experiencing the treasures found in the secret place of the divine.

It's time for us to rise up and utilize the keys we've been given. We must take responsibility as skilled soldiers who know how the war is won. May our lives be pleasing to the One who leads us, and may we live in such a way that produces a garden of the Almighty's blessings.

The kingdom of heaven is like a treasure hidden . . . (Matthew 13:44a)

WORSHIP KEY

1. What Psalms indicate the kind of hunger and thirst David had for God?

2. How did David worship God? What scriptures back up your answer?

3. Read Proverbs 3. Who is the man or woman who is blessed?

4. What keys have you been given?

5. Research the 21st letter of the Hebrew aleph-bet. What have you learned about this Hebrew letter?

9

GARDEN OF DELIGHT

LOVE KEY

And the secret garden bloomed and bloomed and every morning revealed new miracles.

Frances Hodgson Burnett, *The Secret Garden*

In a garden filled with flowers we experience colors, sounds, and scents, as well as inspiration, revelation and delight.

The word paradise refers to a garden. Rabbinical teaching tells us that there are four levels of torah (*Pashat, Remex, Drash and Sod*) and that the acronym for these four levels is *PaRDes*, which is Hebrew for "paradise." The torah is actually the teaching of the law of God as revealed to Moses and recorded in the first five books of the Hebrew scriptures. Eden, as in the Garden of Eden, also known as Paradise, signifies delight. In other words, when we interpret God's instructions and words of truth correctly, our lives can produce a garden of the Almighty's blessings and delight.

There are two Hebrew words that translate to flower: *perach* which means "to break forth, sprout, bud or burst," and *tsuwts*, which evokes images that shine or sparkle. Flowers are a tangible image of beauty and the way they bloom, take root, grow or wither away make them a good image for spiritual themes. Perhaps this is why the tabernacle and temple were filled with flowers. Everything is better in a garden.

The rose is considered to be the most perfect and strongest of all flowers. In chapter 35 of the book of Isaiah, a place called Sharon is mentioned, which is a very large valley-plain. During Solomon's time, Sharon was considered a wild, fertile plain filled with flowers and known for its beauty and majesty, much like a garden might be admired. The phrase "Rose of Sharon" comes out of the Old Testament in the Song of Solomon: "I am the rose of Sharon, and the lily of the valleys" (Song of Solomon 2:1). The term has been used in reference to Jesus, and rightfully so. He is perfect in nature and personality, thus, He can be considered the Rose of Sharon.

In actuality, the person saying she is the "rose of Sharon, and the lily of the valley" is the Shulamite woman, King Solomon's bride. The bride in this passage represents the body of Christ - you and me.

The Shulamite woman knew who she was in the king's presence. Perhaps because of how he looked at her, when she was in the king's presence, she called herself the Rose of Sharon. She was bold enough to speak of her own identity in the face of love, because of his love. It is in God's presence that we find out who we really are. It is in His presence that we awaken with courage.

The master gardener who fulfilled the torah is Jesus. He is the One who helps us to see who were really are by replacing the weed-like lies with truth. Only in the face of the Son are we able to see ourselves, and others, as God sees. In the garden, we come face to face with love that makes us new by changing our thoughts and actions to reflect His love.

In the garden, beauty is unlocked.

In the garden, there is light. It is safe. Life blossoms in the presence of our first love. Jesus is the delight in which our lives will bud, blossom, and shine. And because of His great love for us, He will not allow us to stay entangled in the weeds. His love corrects and redirects to bring about humility instead of pride, and love instead of hate. Beauty can come from ashes, and truth can come instead of lies.

From the beginning, a way was made to come out of the thistles and thorns to enter the garden. Is it really any wonder that so many of us built exquisite forts or sought comfort from enclosed places when we were young?

Even roses that were once withered bloom again in the face of His great love, in the memory where life was taken, or where harsh words were planted. In the right light, life blossoms again, because it has always been destiny to find and cultivate a garden in this great love story.

> Then the green things began to show buds and the buds began to unfurl and show color, every shade of blue, every shade of purple, every tint and hue of crimson.
>
> — - FRANCES HODGSON BURNETT, *THE SECRET GARDEN*

The Greatest Love Story Ever Told

Stories of hope are found in the scriptures, and out of the mouths and pens of the sons and daughters who are speaking up. Those who speak to tell their stories in the boundaries of love, courage, and forgiveness are those who overcome. You, dear one, are an overcomer.

Heroes who overcame, like Deborah and the Samaritan woman, teach us about morality, courage, and redemption. Deborah taught us that in order to go to war and win, we must have discernment, show honor, and wake ourselves up in song. Song that rises up within comes from being in the presence of God, looking to Him, and resting in His presence. The Samaritan woman showed us that we can drink from the living water no matter what we've been through, or what we have put ourselves or others through.

A great story is your own.

With hope and determination, each one of us is in a storyline of defeating the villain. We have One who has gone before us, who causes us to walk in victory in this great love story.

In *The Secret Garden*, that great children's story, the villain was actually the thistles and thorns that came as ugly thoughts of feeling rejected. The war to be won had to do with replacing the lies with truth and love. The way into the garden meant thinking truthful and good thoughts, which ultimately affected the actions of little Mary Lennox.

In reality, the way into the garden has everything to do with truth.

Jesus is the One who changes the common storyline to a remarkable one. He is the Truth. He is the One who cuts away the thistles and thorns and who puts us into a garden where life can grow again. In His presence, healing can take place from the wounds of the past. He teaches us that no matter the oppression or harm that has been done, we can forgive and find healing in doing so.

Jesus, Himself, is the essence of love.

He is the hero, and the only One who leads us into the fullness of restoration. He is the door to the garden. But it's up to each one of us to believe, and then follow Him. Even though I became distracted in my youth and was influenced by deceit, there were good seeds planted deep in the soil of my heart. He was my first love, and in this journey of seeking Him, restoration has been found in everything. Even in some of the darkest memories, there has been healing, because where light shines darkness cannot stay.

We enter into Paradise when we follow the only One worth pursuing. It is God who draws each one of us with loving chords of kindness into the garden. He has already fought for us to come out of the things that keep us unwell, whether it be fear, negativity, unforgiveness, bitterness, addictions, or exploitation.

Moses, a foreshadow of Christ, told the Israelites upon their journey of coming out of Egypt, "The Lord will fight for you; you need only to be still" (Exodus 14:14 NIV). This is the same promise that we can rest in, that God Himself fights for us. It was not the Israelites who fought; rather it was God. And thus they sang, "*Adonai ish milchama,*" which means "The LORD is a man of war; The Lord is His name" (Exodus 15:3 NKJV).

> Let the high praises of God be in their mouth, and *a two-edged sword* in their hand. (Psalm 149:6 *emphasis mine*)

The two-edged sword in our hands is the Word of God. One edge brings life and light and the other cuts proud flesh. The presence of light brings judgement to darkness because darkness cannot exist where light shines. With a two-edged sword in our hands and the praises in our mouths we can wage war in wisdom from a place of rest.

We are told in Matthew 11:12, "From the days of John the Baptist until now the kingdom of heaven suffers violence, and violent men take it by force." To understand the meaning, we must look at the original context. The Hebrew verb *paratz* means "to break forth as a child from the womb." This Hebrew verb resembles action, or breaking forth. To align with and move into the Kingdom of God, we must go through the gate. In John 10:7 we learn that Jesus is that gate: "Very truly I tell you, I am the gate of the sheep."

It was prophesied by Micah in the Old Testament that the Messiah would be the shepherd who would breach a section of the fence or wall of the sheepfold (the earthly existence) for the remnant. The sheep (believers; breachers), would then continue to break through the fence into greener pastures *as they follow their Shepherd*: "He who breaks open the way goes up before them. They break through the gate, and go out. And their king passes on before them, with Yahweh at their head" (Micah 2:13 WEB).

Jesus is both the breaker and the gate (or door) through which His sheep go through to enter into Zion - the New Jerusalem. He made a way for us to break out of entanglements that keep us enslaved. He is the leader in this exodus into the eternal garden. This kind of exodus of breaking forth resembles waging war in wisdom that is reflected by the choices we make.

This kind of *violence* speaks of a soldier who pursues the Kingdom of God no matter the cost.

This kind of *violence* is likened to the one who will speak and act morally according to the living Word of God when it's contradictory to what others are saying or doing who aren't reading their Bibles.

This kind of *violence* is the persistence and boldness it takes to pursue righteousness, justice, and love in the face of wickedness, injustice, and hate.

This kind of *violence* loves people, but slays wickedness.

This kind of *violence* puts to death the desires of the flesh to pursue holiness.

The kind of *violence* does not watch or look at what is vile, which fuels perversion.

This kind of *violence* is for the ones dressed in the right robe, the best robe.

Clothed in the Best Robe

The robe or mantle spoken of in old times was a long garment worn particularly by kings, prophets, nobility, or the rich. This outer garment was the dress of those holding royal or stately rank.

In ancient Israel, a blue sleeveless garment was worn by Jewish priests. Every detail on the high priest's garment was precise. This blue robe had fringe on the lower hem and was adorned with alternating gold bells and pomegranates from blue, purple, and scarlet yarn. The priest in his robe was the only one who could enter the most holy place where the presence of God filled the temple.

The beauty of the priest's robe points to the beauty and excellence of Jesus, our high priest, who presented Himself as a perfect sacrifice. The robe also points to the truth that He gives us a new beginning in righteousness before God, so we can enter the most holy place. The right dress is a robe of covering from the Father. He clothes us, for we "are a chosen people, a royal priesthood, a holy nation, God's special possession" (1 Peter 2:9a NIV).

The color blue is closely associated with the subject of law or commandment. Blue represents the Holy Spirit, living water, and is also the hottest part of the flame. Sapphire blue represents God's nature, His work and His Word, which conforms and transforms us into a reflection of His holy, and divine nature.

A dear friend once said to me, "Jesus' justice is white," which is just one of the reasons why I love the snowfall in Minnesota. The white snow reminds me of the covering over my life and that I am a new creation in Christ, washed clean. An example of this kind of covering can be found in chapter seven of the book of Revelation, where we are given a picture of the throne of God. The scene is of the blood-washed saints from every nation, race, and language, worshiping God.

The prophet Daniel captured in a prophetic word the very distinction of those who are washed clean and dressed properly and those who are not. Those who are not he referenced as acting wickedly, stating, "Many shall purify themselves and make themselves white and be refined, but the wicked shall act wickedly" (Daniel 12:10a ESV). Clearly, this verse highlights the significance of our actions. As God's precious children, we've been given the white robe of redemption, paid for by the blood of the Lamb, Jesus. Our actions are a reflection of our transformation and our love for Him.

We are being refined and defined by the Word, and the greatest commandment is love. "And He said to him, 'You shall love the Lord your God with all your heart, and with all your soul, and with all your mind.' This is the great and foremost commandment. The second is like it, 'You shall love your neighbor as yourself'" (Matthew 22:37-38).

Because of love we are being transformed. We're getting better, instead of bitter. For Daughter Zion, who is now awake, not only does the blue dress fit, but as the warring bride she can sing and dance all the way into the throne room, the garden. She can also use her combat boots to stomp on the serpent along the path, "For the Lord will go before you, And the God of Israel will be your rear guard" (Isaiah 52:12b).

> ...let's make a clean break with everything that defiles or distracts us, both within andwithout. Let's make our entire lives fit and holy temples for the worship of God. (2 Corinthians 7:1b MSG)

Discernment Between Righteousness and Wickedness

We are called to be discerning and recognize the difference between what is wicked and what is holy, and the color purple can teach us just that. Purple is associated with conflicting symbolism and while it is not "evil," it can be mimicked as a representation of what is vile.

Found as a holy example, purple amethyst is the 12th foundation of the New Jerusalem (see Revelation 21:20). The building of the tabernacle in the Old Testament also came with instructions to build with purple.

Before Jesus was crucified, the soldiers tried mocking Him by putting a purple robe on Him. In the book of John, "Pilate then took Jesus and scourged Him. And the soldiers twisted together a crown of thorns and put it on His head, and put a purple robe on Him; and they began to come up to Him and say, 'Hail, King of the Jews!' and to give Him slaps in the face" (John 19:1-2). The irony of the soldiers trying to mock Jesus as being the King of the Jews, is that He really was, and is, the King of the Jews.

Since purple dye was expensive in the ancient world, it became a symbol for power, wealth, and royalty and not particularly a holy example. People can be pushed into a position of fame or false royalty to make a name for themselves by what is vile and evil, leading to attempts to control and ultimately, rebellion against God. This rebellion calls evil "good" and good "evil."

> Do not be deceived, God is not mocked; for whatever a man sows, this he will also reap. For the one who sows to his own flesh will from the flesh reap corruption, but the one who sows to the Spirit will from the Spirit reap eternal life. (Galatians 6:7-8)

Interestingly, the absence of purple trade in the book of Revelation is part of Babylon's fall (18:12). When people stop trading in purple, which represents the world's power, wealth, and "royalty," the city will lose its wealth and power. And when people stop trading with "the souls of men" (18:13) the city has lost its wealth and power. Evil will not be allowed to prevail in the Kingdom of God. Perverse sex, the trafficking of souls, and the false royalty of elevating self will not be allowed.

When Christ comes, He will rule in justice and throw down anything or anyone that opposes Him. Sadly, there are far too many who live as though what they do here on earth doesn't matter, when in fact, it absolutely matters. We will either stand on the side of justice, who is Jesus Christ Himself, or we will be offended by Him who exemplifies love and righteousness.

In these end times, it is important that we awaken to recognize the difference between what is wicked and what is righteous. We must understand how evil operates to deceitfully control, mimic, and entangle. We do not, however, look at evil so intently that it causes us to lose focus. That's what the enemy does - he fights for our attention to distract us from pursuing God.

Jesus washes us and covers us with His righteousness, and with the help of the Holy Spirit, we learn to discern between what is holy and what is wicked. No true believers will ever appear wearing filthy rags of self-righteousness before His throne. We can wear the best robe of His righteousness, if by faith, and through repentance, we've come to Jesus and asked Him to be Lord and Savior, Adonai.

> I will rejoice greatly in the Lord, My soul will exult in my God; For He has clothed me with *garments of salvation,* He has wrapped me with a *robe of righteousness,* As a bridegroom decks himself with a garland, And as a bride adorns herself with her jewels. (Isaiah 61:10, *emphasis mine*)

The Davidic Kingdom

A key indicates control, authority, and entrance.

The term, "Key of David" is referenced in Revelation: "... these are the words of him who is holy and true, who holds the key of David" (3:7). The one who holds the Key of David has control of David's domain - Jerusalem, the city of David, the Kingdom of Israel.

The prophet Isaiah spoke of the symbolism of keys when he prophesied of a day when the true steward would replace the corrupt: "Then I will set the key of the house of David on his shoulder, When he opens no one will shut, When he shuts no one will open" (Isaiah 22:22).

The Davidic Covenant refers to God's promises to David, and thus, Israel. One of those promises was that the Messiah (Jesus Christ), the true steward, would come from the lineage of David and the tribe of Judah. He would be the one to establish a Kingdom that would endure forever. Jesus is the fulfillment of the Davidic Covenant. He is the King who has inherited the throne of His ancestor David, and He has the right to administer and rule over all the affairs of the eternal Kingdom.

A prophecy in the book of Amos declares that God will bring restoration to what has been broken: "In that day I will raise up the fallen booth, and wall up its breaches; I will also raise up its ruins and rebuild it as in the days of old" (Amos 9:11). The booth in this passage refers to the shelter, or tabernacle, of David. To restore the tabernacle of David means to restore what has been broken and ruined and bring it back to the Davidic order of things. One of the ways restoration will be realized is for God's chosen people Israel to no longer be bothered and oppressed:

And I will provide a place for my people Israel and will plant them so that they can have a home of their own and no longer be disturbed. Wicked people will not oppress them anymore, as they did at the beginning. (2 Samuel 7:10 NIV)

With the full restoration of David's governmental rule by King Jesus the Messiah, the future benefits of Davidic order described in Scripture also include:

- World peace (see Isaiah 2:4)
- Universal justice (see Isaiah 9:7)
- The physical presence of King Jesus the Messiah in Jerusalem (see Jeremiah 31:6; Ezekiel 48:35; Isaiah 33:21-22)
- A Temple on Mount Moriah which will also be a house of prayer for all nations with a Jewish flavor (see Isaiah 56:7)
- The *deserts will blossom* like the rose with perennial water sources (see Isaiah 35:1-10)

As we enter into the fullness of the garden of our lives, we are also being prepared to enter eternity. Along the way, with the Messiah, King Jesus as our leader we will learn what it means to subdue, overcome, and conquer. In Zion, a city of promise also known as the New Jerusalem, there will be rest like there once was for Adam and Eve in the garden. The garden that has since been guarded by cherubim and a flaming sword will no longer be hidden from those who have the Lamb's name on their foreheads. The tree of life yielding its twelve kinds of fruit each month will bring healing to the nations (see Revelation 22:2).

· · ·

Keys of Authority and the Song of Awakening

To get on the path of righteousness, which leads into the fullness of the garden, we use our voice in agreement with the Word and align our footsteps with actions of morality, honor and love. In acknowledging Jesus and keeping His Word, there is an open door into the eternal garden: "I know your deeds. Behold, I have put before you an open door which no one can shut, because you have a little power, *and have kept My word, and have not denied My name*" (Revelation 3:8 *emphasis mine*).

With the Word as our lamp, covered in the best robe, we move into the boundary lines of inheritance and out of the culture of Babylon. The alarms are sounding for the sons and daughters to come out of an oppressive system that enslaves to lust, perversion, and greed. In loving Jesus Christ, the Messiah, we keep loyal to His Word: what is pure, what is lovely, and what is true. We recognize and despise what is wicked.

We utilize the keys we have been given, with love as our greatest key of restoration. We bless and pray for Israel, the apple of God's eye and we speak peace to Jerusalem. We worship and bow only to King Jesus, our faithful and triumphant leader. He is the one true God, Adonai - the only one who allows entrance into the garden. Communion, covering and covenant have always been a part of the plan for those clothed in covenant, and created for communion.

Love has a face and a name, and His name is Jesus.

God is building His secret place, His fort, and He is calling His bride into the secret place through truth - *Yeshua Hamashiach,* "Jesus the Messiah." With our hearts set on Him, we move towards destiny, hearing the song that is connecting Heaven and Earth. Like the sound of the loon that carries over a distance to unite lovers, there is a sound of the coming warrior King. We are being drawn towards Him in a song of awakening. This is a wake up call for the final show down before the enemy is cast away for good.

As sons and daughters sing in tune with creation and creation sings in tune with the sons and daughters, a sonic boom will break forth on the eighth day of new beginnings. In that day, He says, "'I will betroth you to Me forever; Yes, I will betroth you to Me in right-eousness and in justice, In lovingkindness and in compassion, And I will betroth you to Me in faithfulness. Then you will know the Lord. It will come about in that day that I will respond,' declares the Lord. 'I will respond to the heavens, and they will respond to the earth, And the earth will respond to the grain, to the new wine and to the oil, And they will respond to Jezreel'" (Hosea 2:19-22).

In that day, Grace and I will continue to sing. The song draws Heaven and Earth together like lightning as all the eternals sing.

Adonai is the Garden

The story of *The Secret Garden* concludes in the same rose garden where Mary found purpose in cultivating the garden. In the end, which was just another beginning, she receives a proposal for marriage and will soon be found in a white wedding dress looking face to face with her beloved. There is no question as to her loyalty of love for her beloved, and his love for her.

Similarly, the greatest love story ever told is coming around full circle from the garden in Eden at the beginning of time, to the garden of gifts in Gethsemane where Jesus laid down His life, to the garden of Golgotha where death was overcome, and all the way to Paradise, the garden of eternal life.

Adonai is leading us into a place of delight where flowers are in bloom and thistles and thorns can not destroy. We can unlock the places of beauty and healing in the garden, because we abide in the vine, Jesus. Through the ministry of the Holy Spirit, we are led through the various seasons of life. He waters us, fills us with His Word for spiritual growth, and at times He takes His Word and prunes us as we go through challenges to remove the dying petals and leaves and the old stubborn flesh.

In the beginning, there was intimacy in a place of delight with no shame or grief and no knowledge of death or destruction. In the garden, there was creativity to cultivate and meet with God face-to-face. He is bringing us back to the beginning, before the violations, the addictions and the hurt, so we can live unhindered, full of life and love. In the great love story we longed for, entwined with God's love and grace, we will someday be united with those we have longed for, seeing them face-to-face.

In the eternal garden, we will come face-to-face with our first love Jesus, within Whom we find complete restoration. He is giving us courage and breathing life by His words. God says, "He who has an ear, let him hear what the Spirit says to the churches. To him who overcomes, I will grant to eat of the tree of life which is in the Paradise of God" (Revelation 2:7).

With such love that He has for us, how can we not form a posture that honors, keep a song on our breath that sustains, make actions that are moral, and have grateful hearts that love unhindered. What hope we have in a King named Jesus!

In the end, or shall we say the new beginning, the sons and daughters of God clothed in the righteousness of Christ not only win, but because of God's lovingkindness, we have been provided with a way back home to paradise, the garden. The way is Jesus Christ, Himself.

Jesus is our greatest hope of restoration, and love is the key to unity.

We've been, and we will be, singing our way into the pearly gates to honor and worship King Jesus, the Messiah Who is faithful and true. A new beginning happens within God's perfect grace that will endure for all of eternity.

In time, destiny unfolds to bring the bride and the Bridegroom together in the greatest love story ever told.

Love, after all, is found in a garden.

The Lord will surely comfort Zion and will look with compassion on all her ruins; he will make her deserts like Eden, her wastelands like the garden of the Lord. Joy and gladness will be found in her, thanksgiving and the sound of singing.

Isaiah 51:3 NIV

LOVE KEY

1. What is the key in chapter nine and who does that lead to? Who is the door to the garden? Identify scriptures to support what you've written.

2. Who is our greatest source of restoration and what scriptures support this truth?

3. Read the scripture from Isaiah at the end of the chapter. How have your wastelands been made to resemble the garden of the Lord? How have your deserts been made like Eden?

4. What has impacted you the most from reading chapter nine? Identity three scripture promises from this chapter. Write them out, say them out loud.

ABOUT THE AUTHOR

DANIELLE FREITAG, LADC serves as the co-founding director of Action169. An overcomer of severe addiction and the commercial sex industry, Danielle works as a counselor and advocate, providing direct support, care and counseling for women in a variety of settings. She is the creator of Arukah, a trauma-informed, faith-centered counseling service promoting holistic restoration through evidence-based practices, including the creative arts. Her mission is to empower women to overcome substance use and to enable those in the strip club industry to know their intrinsic worth.

Offering expert training on combating the realities of exploitation and addiction while providing best care practices, Danielle has been requested to advise medical, government and non-government professionals and churches, both nationally and internationally. Danielle's captivating story of transformation inspires hope and offers solutions.

Corey and Danielle met in the fall of 2008 and were married shortly after, in 2009. The two have had practical and theological training and equipping to provide care services for youth and adults facing challenging life circumstances. In their free time, Corey and Danielle love hiking, traveling and helping others live a healthy lifestyle. They are known for their passionate love of God and desire to carry the message of the good news of Jesus Christ. They reside in Minnesota and serve in leadership positions in ministry as well as throughout the local business community.

ABOUT PHILIP B. HANEY

PHILIP B. HANEY is a founding member of the Department of Homeland Security and served as a Customs and Border Protection officer, retiring honorably in 2015 with 15 years combined federal service. As the president of Venatus Group, Inc. he has been a professional international consultant since 1984.

Haney is the author of *See Something, Say Nothing*, a best-selling exposé of the Obama administration's submission to the goals and policies of the Muslim Brotherhood and other Islamic groups in America and around the world. He has provided classified briefings to both the House and Senate and has been cited in hundreds articles about counter terrorism and national security.

With 45 years experience dealing with counter-terrorism, Haney has traveled more than 20 countries with sustained emphasis & focus on Israel and the Middle East. He has had more than 770 television, radio and speaking appearances including guest spots on the Megyn Kelly and Sean Hannity programs.

Mr. Haney has been a Senior Fellow at the Center for Security Policy since 2015 and was the inaugural recipient of the American Freedom Award from the American Freedom Alliance on May 21, 2017.

ABOUT THE ARTIST

Art has been and continues to be an integral and vital thread interwoven into Anna Friendt's personal story and life journey. It has been a God-given gift that the Lord has used to give her hope from her past and has enabled her to share that same hope with others. God has used artwork in Anna's life to assist in the process of breaking free from depression and anxiety and has provided her a way to heal from a traumatic childhood as well as a troubled young adult life.

Anna uses her work to display Truth. Art is a gift to be shared, which is why she founded *Anchor 13 Studio* - a collaborative studio with a mission of pointing the hearts of people towards the same kind of healing and restoration that she has been able to experience. She is passionate about bringing artists and nonprofits together to promote heart healing and restoration.

Anna's personal artwork can be found via her personal small business, Anna Friendt Artwork & Illustration.

For more information on Anna Friendt please visit anchor13studio.com.

ACTION169

Action169 is built on a foundation of prayer and is committed to ending commercial sexual exploitation and substance use through Christ-centered prevention, intervention and holistic restoration care services.

For speaking inquiries, to host *The Garden Keys* workshop, or for more information on Arukah restoration counseling services, visit the Action169 website.

Action169.com

Info@Action169.com

Bella Daughter

Bella Daughter is an outreach of Action169, a survivor-led organization. Bella Daughter's mission is to love, support and empower women in the sex industry to know their intrinsic worth.

BellaDaughter.com

THE GARDEN KEYS

Unlock Destiny WITH 22 KEYS OF RESTORATION

V.I THE BEGINNING TO ISREAL   V.II AWAKENING DAUGHTER ZION

ACTION169.COM

Book Endnotes and Permissions

1. CHAPTER 1, PAGE 15: *Crown and Throne*, Jon and Jolene Hamill; p.117 ©2013 Burning Lamp Media and Publishing

2. CHAPTER 3, PAGE 45: "Science is clear: Each new human life begins at fertilization," Sarah Terzo for LiveAction; January 13, 2013

3. CHAPTER 4, PAGE 57: "Exodus Cry 2013 Abolition Summit - Enduring Through Brokenness By Dan Allender"

4. CHAPTER 5, PAGE 70: *Prayer: Why Our Words To God Matter* by Corey Russell; p.77, ©2013 Forerunner Publishing, IHOP, Kansas City

5. CHAPTER 6, PAGE 84: *The Jewish Way: Living the Holidays*, by Rabbi Irving Greenberg; p.115 ©1988 Touchstone Publishing

6. CHAPTER 6, PAGE 91: ChaimBentorah.com, *Hebrew Word Study - The Secret Place*, December 9, 2014

7. CHAPTER 7, PAGE 96: The American Heritage® Dictionary of the English Language, Fifth Edition copyright ©2019 by Houghton Mifflin Harcourt Publishing Company. All rights reserved.

8. CHAPTER 7, PAGE 98: *Angel Armies*, Tim Sheets; p.102-103 ©2016 Destiny Image Publishing

9. CHAPTER 7, PAGE 104: *The Deborah Anointing*, Michelle McClaiin-Walters; p.50 ©2015 Charisma House

10. CHAPTER 7, PAGE 106: *Nazirite DNA*, Lou Engle; p. 29 ©2019 Published by Lou Engle Ministries, Inc.

For more info on the Hebrew word definitions and usage found throughout this book, please see The Hebrew-Greek Key Word Study Bible, NASB Revised Edition ©1984, 1990, 2008 by AMG International, Inc.